Modern

Survival

By

Ron Eberhardt

Few people would argue that threats have become all too real. As I sit down to write this book, the United States has suffered multiple incidents. California is currently recovering from an earthquake, Louisiana, a close call with tropical storm Barry, and New York have experienced a failure of its power grid protection system leading to a blackout affecting over 73,000 residences. While this lists a few of the latest incidents currently affecting the country, it in no way considers the threats from wildfire, tornadoes, civil unrest, or any of the other issues we face. The truth is we have built a house of cards that is waiting to collapse upon itself. It is our job to keep the cards up, pick up what falls, and keep moving forward.

Our country's infrastructure, for the most part, is antiquated, beginning with the electrical grid. It doesn't take much for our electrical grid to stop working. Some places see the electricity going out regularly while others it's only occasionally. It might be a planned outage or not. Our other infrastructures, such as those controlling water, sewer, communication, and transportation, can be just as problematic.

But how can we survive without our modern way of life? There is something to be said for our ability to ask Google a question, order products from Amazon, get news anytime we want it, or any of the other benefits that many of us take for granted. As a whole, we have been lucky to be born into this life, the world we know, where we work and play, and for the most part, I wouldn't have it any other way.

As I type on my computer to bring you this book, my goal is to give you some knowledge that may help combat the threats you may face in the wake of a disaster. Everyone may have different risk factors based on where they live. Specific risks are higher in cities than in rural areas, and others that rural areas face every day and cities will never see. Some threats that neighborhoods don't need to concern themselves with others may mark as their highest risk. Then there are risk factors that everyone will face. No matter what the risk is, you must work to eliminate and reduce the effects of those you encounter.

That's where this book comes in.

Unlike books that try to tell you to move out to the country and build an underground bunker to hide in, I'll try to impart some practical techniques and approaches to preparedness. We will discuss when you should bug-out or evacuate and times to dig in and weather the storm based on where you are and what the threat is.

While I hope that everything you read here remains nothing more than good-to-know information that you never have to use, the truth is many of you will someday have to decide what to do in an emergency. Even if you manage to avoid any catastrophic events, you will more than likely have a power outage, see some severe weather, witness a car wreck with injuries, or have a family member or friend in dire need. These are just part of being here on this great planet.

In reading this book, you will learn how to store food and water for emergencies, perform a risk analysis, understand how to create different survival and bug-out kits to quickly get you on your way if you have to evacuate, and maybe a few other things along the way; ensuring your family's security and safety.

Ron Eberhardt

Table of Contents

Are You Prepping for the Right Threats?

It is difficult to prepare if you don't know what threats and why you should. Some people are prepping for the Martian zombie horde to attack, but don't have a simple blackout kit or some food available if the power goes out.

Sure, it's fun to plan for the worst-case scenario, but if you don't live by a large body of water, you probably don't need to worry about a tsunami wiping out your house. Let's begin with some of the most common threats we face. You can divide these threats into three potential categories: natural or Mother Nature, human-made, and technological.

Threats

Natural Threats

Severe Weather

Regardless of where you live, the weather will affect you and usually in more than one way.

Winter Storms

Throughout the world, cold temperatures and heavy snowfall affect numerous regions. Some of these areas will see feet (meters) of snow instead of inches (centimeters). The winter of 2017-2018 will go down in the history books as one of the longer ones starting in October and continuing through Mid-April with a parade of winter storms blasting the East Coast into March, a record-setting snowfall in the South.

2018 saw an epic onslaught of four straight Nor'easters in March with a barrage of high-impact winter storms beginning during the first three weeks.   Winter
storms Riley, Quinn, Skylar, and Toby brought heavy snow, gusty winds, and coastal flooding to parts of the mid-Atlantic and Northeast.

Winter Storm Quinn is remembered for its heavy snow putting more than a million along the I-95 Northeast corridor in the dark when 20 inches of snow fell in seven states. Winter Storm Riley was responsible for stalling ground and air traffic, forcing the closure of numerous schools, and caused a blackout affecting over two million residents. The coastal area of Massachusetts experienced severe coastal flooding, beach erosion, and seawall breaches. Winter Storm Skylar brought blizzard conditions knocking out power to virtually all of Nantucket Island. Boston and Worcester, Massachusetts, each set new one-day March snowfall records. Then last, but not least, Winter Storm Toby brought one of the most massive spring snowstorms to parts of the mid-Atlantic, including Philadelphia and Washington, D.C. Toby dumped a foot or more of snow in five states from New York's Long Island to southern West Virginia.

Fortunately, we usually have some warning before storms such as those listed above hit. In fact, due to advances in meteorology, forecasters can often predict these storms several days if not over a week in advance of them hitting our area. By paying attention to weather forecasts and acting accordingly, you will have plenty of time to stay on top of the situation, ensure you have the supplies you need, and avoid that dreaded last-minute trip to the store.

Action Recommendation:

The first step is gaining knowledge and knowing your area's risk for winter storms before the fact. Having this knowledge will help you prepare before the effects of the winter storm affect your area, and there is a run on the store.

Extreme winter weather can leave communities without power or other services for long periods. If a winter storm is a risk for your area, you need to prepare your home and family to keep out the cold by completing the following steps:

1. Insulate your home using additional insulation, caulking, and weather stripping
2. Wrap your pipes to stop them from freezing where necessary
3. Install and test both smoke alarms and carbon monoxide detectors. They should have battery backups to ensure they are

operable. Change the batteries in all detectors twice a year. Most people do this when they change their clocks for daylight savings.

4. Pay attention to your local weather reports and warnings of freezing weather and winter storms

After knowledge, having what is needed to keep you warm is essential. You should create a blackout kit for your home, a car kit for your car, and a 72-hour bag for each member of your family. If you have pets, you will want a pet kit designed for each.

Gather supplies to stay home for several days without power while keeping in mind the specific needs of everyone in your group, including medical needs and medication. Do not forget the needs of your pets. Often they are overlooked when making emergency plans.

Have extra batteries for radios and flashlights. Create an emergency supply kit for your vehicle. Include jumper cables, sand, a flashlight, warm clothes, blankets, bottled water, and non-perishable snacks. Keep the gas tank full.

During a winter storm, safety should be utmost in your mind; most people get in trouble because of decisions they make in those weather conditions. You should stay off the roads and limit your time outside. If you must go out, then ensure you wear layers of warm clothing and watch for signs of frostbite and hypothermia.

Sites that I frequently use to monitor the weather include:

The National Weather Service at www.weather.gov
The National 7-Day Significant Fire Potential at
https://psgeodata.fs.fed.us/forecast/
NOAA Alerts and Warnings at
https://alerts.weather.gov/

Heat Waves

Heatwaves can be extremely severe, especially to the elderly, young, and ill. Excessively high temperatures that continue over several days or weeks put considerable strain on the electrical grid, as well as having a significant impact on people throughout the area.

As those living in this area begin to crank up their air conditioners in hopes of getting cooled down, brownouts and blackouts start becoming commonplace. The heat will also start to put a strain on our bodies as it begins affecting our sleep patterns leading to people becoming excessively tired and agitated. This stress can then lead to an increase in fights and other violent acts. For those that are sensitive, heatwaves can also cause significant medical concerns. Address any medical concerns before those conditions become unmanageable.

Action Recommendation:

If under an EXTREME HEAT WARNING, it is essential to find air conditioning and stay cool by avoiding strenuous activities, wearing light clothing, and drinking plenty of fluids. Before the heatwave hits, you should prepare your home to keep cool by:

1. Covering windows with drapes or shades
2. Using weather-stripping on doors and windows

3. Window deflectors, such as aluminum foil-
    covered cardboard to reflect heat outside
4. Adding insulation to keep the heat out
5. Using attic fans to clear hot air
6. Installing window air conditioners and
    insulating around them

During a Heat Wave, never leave a child, adult, or animal alone inside a vehicle on a warm day. Every year we see on the news a child or pet dying after being left in a hot car. Remember, regardless of how hot it is outside, the heat is intensified by the windows in the car.

If you're outside, find shade. Wear loose, lightweight, and light-colored clothing; and drink plenty of fluids to stay hydrated.

Droughts

Droughts are a normal part of the planet's climate cycle caused by a shortage of water over an extended period. They occur in all climate zones and can either be short or span multiple years.

There have been three significant droughts affecting the United States in the last 100 years. Two of these include the 1930s Dust Bowl and the 1950s drought. Each of these lasted 5-7 years and affected large regions with devastating results.

Although not as dynamic as other disasters, droughts can be among the costliest weather-related events with the most far-reaching effects. Between 1980–2014, there were 22 drought events with losses exceeding $1 billion (CPI-Adjusted) each across the United States.

Though we can't prevent droughts, we can reduce some of the issues related by watching things we do out of habit. We should always be responsible for how we use our water sources and work to ensure that they are around for as long as possible through using rain barrels and water conservation techniques.

Floods

Floods may be the most common natural disaster in the United States. Flooding may occur when water overtops or breaks through levees along rivers, or due to an accumulation of rainwater on saturated ground. Floods cause damage to homes and businesses in the natural floodplains of rivers. Some develop slowly, while others can occur in minutes and without signs of rain. Additionally, they can be local, impacting a neighborhood or community, or very large, affecting entire river basins.

In 2019 we saw damaging floods throughout the Midwest and South leading to evacuations in Oklahoma, Louisiana, Georgia, Alabama, and many other states. After Barry hit, flooding affected Arkansas Police Stations, Animal Shelter, and washed out highways. These incidents of flooding can last anywhere from hours to weeks, depending on the cause and may incur millions of dollars in damage.

Failing to evacuate, entering flood waters, or remaining after a flood has passed may result in injury or death.

Action Recommendation:

As with everything else, your safety begins with knowing types of flood risk in your area. Once you know your risk learn and practice your evacuation routes, know where shelters are, and the flash flood response plan. Gather supplies in one place so you can leave immediately, or if your services are cut off. Most of your needed supplies should be kept in your bug-out-bag. Keep in mind any specific needs each person in your group may have, including medication. Don't forget the needs of your pets.

Purchase or renew a flood insurance policy. Policies can take as long as 30 days to go into effect and can protect the life you've built. Homeowner's policies do not cover flooding. Put together your preparedness thumb drive and keep essential documents in a waterproof container. Move valuables to higher levels. Declutter drains and gutters. Install check valves and consider a sump pump with a battery.

If you receive an immediate flood warning, go to a safe location previously identified. If told to evacuate, do so immediately. Never drive around barricades or walk, swim, or drive through floodwaters. Stay off bridges over fast-moving water. They can wash away without warning. If your car gets trapped in rapidly moving water, stay inside. If the water begins to rise inside the vehicle, seek refuge on top of the car's roof.
If in a building during a flood, go to the highest floor but never climb into a closed attic. You may become trapped by rising floodwater. Go on the roof only if necessary. Once on the roof, begin to signal for help.

After the incident, you should listen to authorities for information and instructions, return home only when authorities say it is safe, and avoid driving, except in emergencies.

Tornadoes

The morning of March 3rd, 2019, saw a significant weather event affecting the South over 6 hours a total of 41 tornadoes touching down across portions of Alabama, Georgia, Florida, and South Carolina. The most violent and devastating of these tornados, an EF-4, roared through eastern Alabama, killing 23 people and injuring over 100 others. At one point, this massive tornado had a wind speed estimated at 170 mph and measured four times wider than an average funnel, as it moved across Lee County. This Tornado was the first EF-4 tornado to hit the U.S. since one that hit Van Zandt County, Texas, on April 29, 2017.

Tornadoes are rapidly rotating air columns in contact with both the surface and a cumulonimbus cloud. They are a common occurrence throughout the Midwest, though it seems that we are seeing them more often in other locations.

Most tornadoes have wind speeds that are less than 110 miles per hour, are approximately 250 feet across, they usually travel only a few miles before they dissipate. The most extreme have been known to attain wind speeds over 300 miles per hour, and measure more than two miles in diameter staying on the ground for dozens of miles.

One of the problems with tornadoes is the lack of warning time before they strike. Often, there are only minutes to react before the storm hits the area with the warning. Fortunately, tornadoes can be detected as they form through the use of Pulse-Doppler radar by recognizing patterns in velocity and reflectivity data, as well as through the efforts of storm spotters and storm chasers.

Tornado Enhanced Fujita Scale		
F-Number	Wind	Damage
F-0	65-85 mph	Light Damage
EF-1	86-110 mph	Moderate Damage, Damage to Roofs
EF-2	111-135 mph	Significant Damage, Roofs Torn Off
EF-3	136-165 mph	Severe Damage, Houses Missing Walls
EF-4	166-200 mph	Devastating Damage, Houses Leveled
EF-5	>200 mph	Extreme Damage, Houses Disintegrated

Action Recommendation:

If you receive a Tornado Warning, immediately go to a safe location and take additional cover by shielding your head and neck. Place materials such as furniture and blankets around you to further protect you. Listen to your local emergency alert service, NOAA Weather Radio, or other local alerting systems for current emergency information and instructions.

Never attempt to outrun a tornado. If you are in your car or outdoors and cannot get to a building, look for a protected area. Add further protection by covering your head and neck with your arms and cover your body with a coat or blanket, if possible.

Cyclone Activity
(Hurricanes, Typhoons and Tropical Storms)

On August 23rd, 2005, a Tropical Depression which would soon become Tropical Storm Katrina originated over the Bahamas. On August 25th, Katrina strengthened into a hurricane two hours before making landfall at Hallandale Beach and Aventura. Katrina was degraded to a tropical storm then emerging into the Gulf of Mexico on August 26th, making its second landfall in southeast Louisiana as a Category 3 hurricane on the 29th. This time Katrina was responsible for severe destruction ranging from central Florida to Texas, much due to the storm surge

and levee failure. Eighty percent of New Orleans and large tracts of neighboring parishes became flooded. Floodwater lingered for weeks, killing 1,400 due to levee failure. America was forever changed.

Whether we call them hurricanes over the Atlantic and Eastern Pacific or Typhoons over the Western Pacific, Tropical Cyclones are the most violent storms on Earth, forming over warm ocean waters near the equator.

Tropical cyclones require warm, moist air as fuel, which, therefore, tropical cyclones form only in regions where ocean water is a minimum of 80 degrees Fahrenheit for at least the top 165 feet below the surface. Warm water by itself won't form a tropical cyclone. A hurricane needs wind, as the wind passes over the ocean's surface, water evaporates and rises this water vapor then cools and condenses back into large water droplets, forming large cumulonimbus clouds. These clouds are just the beginning. The storm must maintain wind speeds above 74 mph, be at least 50,000 ft high, and around 125 miles across to be a hurricane.

Tropical cyclone categories:

Category	Wind Speed (mph)	Damage at Landfall
1	74-95	Minimal
2	96-110	Moderate
3	111-129	Extensive
4	130-156	Extreme
5	157 or higher	Catastrophic

No discussion of hurricanes would be complete without mentioning one of the most devastating events in memorable history, Hurricane Katrina. Even with the warnings repeatedly given, more than 1,800 people caught in the hurricane's path lost their lives.

These tropical storms and cyclones, fortunately, don't just appear; they can be tracked days out from making landfall. By acting on these reports early, you will have ample time to make necessary preparations to include securing your home, and if needed, evacuating to a safer location.

Sites I frequently use to monitor weather are:

National Hurricane Center website at https://www.nhc.noaa.gov/

Action Recommendation:

If under a Hurricane Warning, find shelter. Finding shelter can include evacuating if you have time or taking refuge in a designated storm shelter or interior room if you do not have time to leave.

36 hours from arriving

If you haven't done so yet, begin monitoring the
location and threat of the Hurricane.
Perform an inventory and restock your emergency
preparedness kit as needed. Include at least seven
days of food and water, medications, a flashlight,
batteries, cash, and first aid supplies. All of these
items should already be part of your 72-hour or
bug-out-bag. Also, bookmark your city or county
emergency alert website on your phone and
computer or tablet for quick access to storm
updates and emergency instructions.

Have a communication plan that includes how to
communicate with family members if you lose
power. For example, you can text message, or use
your social media. During disasters, a text message
is usually more reliable and faster than making
phone calls because phone lines are often
overloaded. Only call in the case of an immediate
emergency.

Review your evacuation zone, your evacuation route, and shelter locations. Discuss your evacuation plan with your family. You may have to leave quickly, so ensure everyone understands your evacuation plan. Ensure your car is ready to go with the gas tank full; stock your vehicle with emergency supplies and a change of clothes.

Get your home ready; if you have flood insurance, your policy may cover up to $1000 in items to help protect your insured property. You should keep copies of any receipts and a record of the time you spent performing the work to safeguard your property. These should be submitted to your insurance adjuster when you file your claim.

18-36 hours from arriving

Start safeguarding your home by bringing loose, lightweight objects that could become projectiles in high winds inside; also anchor objects that would be unsafe to bring inside; and trim or remove trees close enough to fall on your home.

Cover all windows though permanent storm shutters offer the best protection. If you don't have storm shutters, a good option is to board up your windows with 5/8" plywood. These should be previously cut to fit and ready to install over your windows when you need to.

6-18 hours from arriving

Turn on your TV or check your city/county website every 30 minutes to get the latest weather updates and emergency instructions. Ensure your cell phone battery remains at 100% as long as possible by plugging it in to ensure a fully charged battery if there's a power outage.

6 hours from arriving

If you're not in an evacuation area, plan to stay where you are and let friends and family know you are safe and where you are.

Finish getting your home ready by closing your storm shutters or finish boarding up your windows and stay away from windows. Place your refrigerator and freezer on its coldest setting and open only if necessary. If you lose power, the food will last longer if the door stays shut. Keep a thermometer in your fridge to check the food temperature when the power comes back on.

Turn on your TV or check your city/county website every 30 minutes to get the latest weather updates and emergency instructions.

Earthquakes

At 5:03 p.m. on October 17, 1989, the San Francisco Bay Area was buzzing about baseball. With both teams in the World Series from the Bay Area, it was the battle of the Bay. The third game of the series, with Oakland leading by two games, was scheduled to begin around 5:30 p.m. at San Francisco's Candlestick Park. With the stadium-filling, cameras going live on the field, 5:04 p.m.

struck, and so did a magnitude 6.9 earthquake that rocked the San Francisco Bay region. Though the stadium held up to the shaking, other parts of the Bay Area were not as fortunate with Fisherman's Wharf collapsing into the sea and the upper deck of the Bay Bridge collapsing on the lower, pinning numerous cars and people beneath it. Sixty-seven people perished, and more than 3,000 others injured as a result of the quake, which lasted around 15 seconds.

With the Loma Prieta, Northridge, Tohoku and Christchurch Earthquakes, the first many people think of when thinking of earthquakes, it's no wonder that many feel this is something that affects the Pacific Ring of Fire. While the Ring of Fire, to include California, Japan, Hawaii, and Alaska, is the best known for earthquakes, earthquakes can happen anywhere. Earthquakes strike without warning and can cause significant loss of life and property damage.

What is known is that these earthquakes happen along fault lines where the plates move along or under each other. Unfortunately, there is typically little to no warning before an earthquake occurs. The lack of notice makes it even more essential to take the necessary steps to prevent items from falling off shelves and walls and make your house earthquake ready if you are in an earthquake-prone location.

Richter Scale	
Richter Magnitude	Earthquake Effect
0-2	Not Felt by People
2-3	Felt Little by People
3-4	Ceiling Lights Swing Items May Fall off Shelves or Walls
4-5	Walls Crack
5-6	Furniture Moves
6-7	Some Buildings Collapse
7-8	Many Buildings Destroyed
8-UP	Destruction of Buildings, Bridges, and Roads

A site that I frequently use to monitor earthquake Risks:

The USGS at https://www.usgs.gov/

Action Recommendation:

Since there is no warning before an earthquake can strike, it is essential that if you live in an at-risk area, you prepare before it happens. To protect yourself and your family, start by securing large furniture, refrigerators, televisions, and any objects that hang on walls. Store any heavy and breakable objects on lower shelves.

Have a family emergency communications plan that includes an out-of-state point of contact — Plan where to meet if your group gets separated.
Make a supply kit including enough food and water for a minimum of three days, a flashlight, fire

extinguisher, and a whistle in case you get trapped. Consider each person's specific needs, both medical and personal, including medication.

Keep extra batteries for any device that takes them and charging devices for phones and other critical equipment.

Keep in mind the needs of your pets and service animals, keeping extra food and water for them. Keep extra leashes for your pets in your bug-out-bag also.

Consider keeping an earthquake insurance policy if you live in an earthquake-prone area. A standard homeowner's insurance policy will not cover earthquake damage. Consider making improvements to your building to fix structural issues that could cause your building to collapse during an earthquake.

Tsunamis

On the morning of March 11th, 2011, there was a massive earthquake, with a magnitude of 9.0, 43 miles east of the Oshika Peninsula. It is the most powerful earthquake ever recorded in Japan. The earthquake caused multiple other disasters, including the Fukushima nuclear disaster in Okuma, Fukushima Prefecture of Japan. The quake also triggered a powerful tsunami with waves that reached heights of up to 133 ft in Miyako, a part of Tōhoku's Iwate Prefecture, and which, in

the Sendai area, traveled at 435 mph for up to
6 miles inland. Residents of Sendai had only ten
minutes warning before the tsunami reached
them.

As of 2019, the latest report from the
Japanese National Police confirmed 15,897 deaths,
6,157 injuries, and 2,532 people missing across
twenty prefectures, and a report from 2015
indicated 228,863 people were still displaced.

With events such as the Sumatra Tsunami on
December 26th, 2004, and the North Pacific Coast
in Japan on March 11th, 2011, massive tsunamis
are still fresh in many of our minds.

If a tsunami-causing incident occurs close to the
coastline, a tsunami can reach coastal communities
within minutes. Even small tsunamis (only 6 feet in
height) can form strong currents. These current are
capable of knocking someone off their feet and
severely injure them or carry them off to sea.

The U.S. Tsunami Warning Centers, working in
conjunction with USGS seismic networks, help
determine when and where to issue tsunami
warnings to warn people of potential threats.

If you receive a tsunami warning, feel strong
shaking at the coast or see unusual wave activity
such as the sea withdrawing far from shore, move
to high ground and stay away from the beach until
wave activity has subsided (usually several hours to
days).

Action Recommendation:

If you find yourself under a Tsunami warning,
evacuate immediately do not wait.

Sites I frequently use to monitor weather are:

The U.S. Tsunami Warning System at
https://www.tsunami.gov/

Wildfires

California is known for its wildfires, and it seems that these fires are becoming ever more devastating, with 2018 being the most catastrophic fire season for California to date. Fires such as the Camp, Holy, and Woolsey fires marked 2018 as one of the deadliest fire seasons on record with the Camp Fire killing at least 88 civilians, injuring at least three firefighters, and destroying more than 10,321 structures.

Every year, fires break out along the West Coast of the United States, driven by low humidity and strong winds. These Wildfires cause massive damage as well as threaten the lives of thousands of residents.

Various causes, including arson, unattended campfires, fireworks, cigarettes, cars, and power lines, have contributed to this increase in the number of fires.

While residents in these areas understand the threat, they face and may receive warnings ahead of time when conditions are becoming dangerous, a significant part of the danger from wildfire is the speed it can move in, its' ability to change directions based on terrain and wind changes, and its' ability to spot miles ahead of itself.

Action Recommendation:

If you find yourself dealing with wildland fire, you find yourself in danger as the fire can be quick moving and overtake areas within minutes. So, what do you do? First, evacuate when told to leave. Every year evacuations go out, and people decide to stay and defend their property, and while I can understand someone wanting to stay and protect what they have, I also know that this action places both the person deciding to stay and firefighters at risk. That is why I must repeat if you are told to leave, do so. If you are trapped, call 911, explain where you are, and mark the building or area you are in so firefighters can reach you quickly. When evacuating, use N95 masks and safety glasses or sunglasses to protect you and your family from particles in the air.

Before the incident:

Sign up for your community's warning system or reverse 911. The Emergency Alert System (EAS) and Local Radio Channels will also provide emergency alerts. These warnings, as well as watching the news for fire activity in your area, will help ensure that you are ready and prepared for any fires that may become a threat.

Before Fire Season even begins, sit down with a map and identify evacuation locations and routes in each direction from where you are. Drive the roads and find shelter locations along each in case you do have to pull over or abandon your car. Have a plan to meet with family members that may be elsewhere if you receive an evacuation order, also have a plan to evacuate your animals.

Gather emergency supplies, supplies need to include N95 respirator masks to filter out particles from the air, safety Glasses, gloves, long sleeve

shirts, pants, and boots. Keep in mind specific
needs for each person in your family,
including medication. Don't forget the needs of your
pets.

Clothing should be cotton, Nomex, or other material
that will not melt if exposed to heat. Do not use
polyester or anything with plastics in it.

In case, you may need to shelter in place,
designate a room that can be closed off from the
outside air. Close all windows and doors if you can
set up a portable air cleaner to keep down indoor
pollution levels.

Keep essential documents in a fireproof safe place
and keep copies at an alternate location as well as
create a password-protected digital copy of these
documents on a thumb drive.

Create a defensible space free of leaves, debris, or
flammable materials for at least 30 feet from your

home. Find an outside water source and hose. The hose needs to reach any area of your property.

To design your area and create defensible space, assess both the horizontal and vertical aspects of the vegetation surrounding your home. Thin your bushes and trees, so the crowns do not intersect, and there is space between each. To avoid the fire from spreading vertically, prune the lowest tree branches to maintain a vertical separation from the top of grass and bushes from tree branches.

Begin preparing your area by creating three zones around your home. Base the size of your zones on the fire threat in your area. The zone closest to your home will have the greatest need for fuel modification with progressively fewer changes needed in the other two zones.

Begin by attempting to eliminate all combustible materials within 30 feet of your home. Include any fire-prone vegetation, firewood stacks, flammable patio furniture, and dimensioned lumber decking. To reduce flammability, try to use irrigated grass, rock gardens, stone patios, metal patio furniture, and noncombustible decking in this zone. Before the start of the fire season, remove combustible litter on your roof and from your gutters, trim any branches that overhang the roof and chimney.

In your Zone 2, plant fire-resistant vegetation that retains moisture well and requires minimum maintenance. Separate any structures such as a detached garage, pump house, pergola, and utility shed from your home by at least 50 feet. Increase the distance past 50 feet if the building stores combustible materials. Ensure that your patio furniture is metal or at least non-flammable and, if possible, kept at least 30 feet from any structure. Store patio furniture in a protected location, such as a garage or shed. Place woodpiles at least 30 feet from any building, storing the wood in a vegetation-free graveled area. Store any fuel tanks you have away from structures, underground, or on a cement pad.

In Zone 3, reduce any fuels farther than 100 feet from the building by thinning and pruning vegetation horizontally and then vertically. The goal is to improve the health of the wildlands and help slow an approaching wildfire.

During the Incident:

If you receive an evacuation order, evacuate, and if trapped, call 911. Leaving as soon as you receive an evacuation order may be what keeps you alive during a worst-case scenario. It may not be your life that you are placing in jeopardy by staying. Whether it is an evacuation advisory, warning, or order, if you do not feel safe and can evacuate, do so.

If you do shelter in place. Move to a previously designated interior room that can be closed off.

Close all of your doors and windows. Set up your portable air cleaner and mark the outside of the building. This will let rescue workers know someone is sheltering in the building.

Regardless if you decide to evacuate or shelter in place. If you find yourself trapped by the fire, take these steps to increase your chances of survival. First, know what to expect; remember that the roar of a wildfire can be loud. Your house will get very hot and smoky as the fire front passes. Ensure you are emotionally prepared to deal with the horrific sound and strong natural urge to flee. If you run at this point, you will not outrun the fire and, unfortunately, be placing yourself in a worst-case scenario. Although it will be scorching, it can be four or five times worse outside.

As the fire approaches, close all windows and doors, placing wet towels under the door and window openings. Close your window blinds and remove any flammable window treatments, move furniture away from windows and sliding glass doors, shut off attic fans, whole-house fans, swamp coolers, and interior fans to keep the smoke and ash from being drawn into the structure. Shutting these fans off and shutting off open areas of your home should reduce the smoke coming into the house and allow you to breathe easier. Put on your personal protective equipment. This should include an M95 mask, glasses, gloves, long sleeve shirt, pants, and hiking boots.

Be ready to fight the fire, having your fire extinguishers and garden hoses available to use; fill anything that can hold water(sinks, tubs, and buckets) with water for extinguishing any embers that may enter or land on your home. Wet or remove swamp-cooler pads to prevent them from catching fire.

Place your sprinklers in areas where they can soak your shelter and surroundings, and turn them on. Set hoses in easily reachable areas protected from flames, keeping them ready to use once the front of the fire has passed.

Plan for the loss of power, having flashlights and batteries ready. Disconnect electric garage door openers so that you can operate doors manually.

Bring your pets inside, placing them in their carriers ready to leave. If you do have livestock or horses, place them in an irrigated pasture or area without a large number of fuels. Have your horse trailer ready to evacuate as soon as it is safe to do.

Leave your exterior and interior lights on to help firefighters find your home in dense smoke. Close exterior doors and windows but do not lock them so rescue workers can gain access if needed.

Remain in the center of your home, away from windows and glass doors.

Close or cover outside attic, eaves, and vents preventing embers from entering.

If you did evacuate but are now trapped in your vehicle. A structure will offer more protection than your car, if there is a nearby building, get inside. If there isn't a building, try to find a large open area, park, and stay in your car where it will be safer than being in the open. Make your vehicle more visible in smoke by turning on your headlights. Close all of your car windows and doors, shut off air vents and turn off the air conditioner. Place your protective clothing and mask on, and get under blankets or coats, preferably wool if possible, and lie on the floor. Once the fire front passes and the outside temperature cools, get out and go to a safe area that has already burned.

After the fire has passed:

After the fire passes, listen to authorities to find out when it is safe to return. Do not return until the evacuation warning has lifted. It is still very dangerous as there may be pockets that can burn you, your pets, or start another fire.

It is essential to let your family and friends know you are safe, but send text messages or social media to reach out to loved ones instead of trying to make calls on your cell phone.

Wear a NIOSH certified-respirator (dust mask)

Wet any debris to minimize breathing dust particles. Document property damage with photographs, conduct an inventory and contact your insurance company for assistance.

Sites I frequently use to monitor fires include:

The National Interagency Fire Center at https://www.nifc.gov/

The National Geographic Area Coordination Center
at https://gacc.nifc.gov/

YubaNet Fire News at https://yubanet.com/Fires/

Volcanoes

When volcanoes erupt, they can cause tremendous damage and significant loss of life and property.

These eruptions can occur continuously, such as can be seen in Hawaii or with massive simultaneous damage, such as seen in 1980 at Mt St Helens. On May 18th, 1980, at 8:32 am, Mt St Helens in Washington erupted, killing 57 people, most from asphyxiation after inhaling hot ash. Even in the case of volcanoes that have been erupting for some time, a threat still exists and should be monitored. For instance, Hawaii's Kilauea volcano erupting since 1983 became more dangerous on May 3rd, 2018, with an increase in lava flows damaging residential neighborhoods and forcing over 2,000 people to evacuate their homes.

A well-known threat is the Famous Yellowstone Caldera. Underneath the famous Yellowstone National Park lies a supervolcano that last erupted around 640,000 years ago, launching approximately 240 cubic miles of ash and debris into the atmosphere.

These and other incidents, continue to highlight the threat volcanoes pose.

Action Recommendation:

To begin with, understand if you are in an area affected by this threat. For the most part, if you are, you will know as you really can't miss a volcano. The Volcano Notification Service will provide up-to-date information about eruptions. If the volcano is showing increased activity, you need to be ready to evacuate and follow evacuation orders from local authorities. Remember to leave early and stay alive. While going avoid areas downwind and river valleys downstream of the volcano. Wind and gravity can and will carry rubble and ash.

Use long sleeve shirts, pants, boots, and face mask to protect yourself from falling ash that can irritate skin and injure breathing passages, eyes, and open wounds. Choose a well-fitting, certified face mask such as an N95 and avoid driving in heavy ashfall.

Sites I recommend using to monitor volcanoes include:

The Volcano Hazards Program at
https://volcanoes.usgs.gov/index.html

Solar Flares

While not a top priority in most risk assessments, solar flares cause real issues, as seen in September 1859, when a powerful Solar Flare caused a geomagnetic storm wreaking havoc on the telegraph system, or March 13th, 1989 when the entire province of Quebec, Canada went dark. On March 13, just after 2:44 a.m, a Magnetic Disturbance caused by a solar flare found a weakness in the electrical power grid of Quebec. During the 12-hour blackout that followed, millions of people found themselves in dark office buildings, underground pedestrian tunnels, and stalled elevators. The outage also closed schools and businesses, kept the Montreal Metro shut down during the morning rush hour, and closed Dorval Airport.

With us moving to a more computerized society, such a flare or storm today could result in catastrophic consequences.

Action Recommendation:

Preparing for solar flares includes being ready for a power surge, solar shielding, and preparing for a power outage. We will cover preparing for a power outage in the electrical grid collapse section.

Surge Protectors: A powerful solar storm may cause significant power surges that may fry anything in its path. Therefore you need to protect your electronics by using surge protectors and unplugging electronic devices when they are not in use.

- **Whole House Surge Protector:** This type of surge protector will connect to your home's breaker panel providing protection from power surges.
- **Individual Surge Protectors:** For added protection, install surge protectors on computers, TVs, stereos, and other electronics in your home.
- **Unplug Electronic Devices:** Unplugging your electronic devices will ensure they aren't damaged by a power surge.

Shielding from Solar Radiation: We don't know the full effects of solar radiation. If you've ever searched the internet for solar flares, you've found all levels of paranoia and information on everything from shielding yourself and your home from radiation, with all manner of solutions. Short of some radical measures, it doesn't hurt to be prepared.

A simple way to shield electronics from electromagnetic radiation is with a Faraday cage. A Faraday cage is simple to build using a cardboard box and wrapping it with aluminum foil. Another easy solution is to line the inside of a metal garbage can with cardboard. During peak radiation storms, it's a simple matter to put your small electronics inside and close the lid.

Technological Threats

Electrical Grid Collapse

The Power Grids spanning the United States are antiquated and, in most areas, very fragile. With everything from climate control to keeping food fresh, transportation, and much more relying on our Electrical Grid, power outages can range from being an annoyance to a matter of life and death. Power outages often accompany severe weather, fires, and other disasters we speak about in this book.

A typical outage can last a few hours to a couple of days, and with minor planning, it usually won't cause much hardship. However, more prolonged outages can lead to heating or cooling, food preparation, and even security issues.

Action Recommendation:

The most common threat many of us will face is a power outage that might take some time to repair. You can prepare for this the way you'd get ready for any kind of storm by stocking up on supplies that don't take electricity from the grid. You will also need to take some additional steps to ensure that parts of your everyday life that do need power remain in tack.

Do this by ensuring you have the following:

- **Blackout kit:** Create a blackout kit with flashlights, batteries, cooking and heating fuel, battery-powered, radio, external battery for your cell phone tablet, or anything else you may need, first-aid kit, food, and clean water.
- **Back up of essential documents:** Consider a backup stash with paper copies of

financial and personal records, cash, road maps, address book, and anything else you'd need if your handy digital gizmos are out of commission for a while.

- **Battery Backup for Computers:** An Uninterrupted Power Supply (UPS) looks a lot like a standard surge protector but contains batteries that keep computers running smoothly without damage during power fluctuations and brownouts.
- **Off the Grid Power:** Buy a generator and extra fuel, or install a backup energy supply such as solar panels.

Supply Shortages

Anyone that has been through a major storm, hurricane, or other crises can tell you that when things get bad, the stores run out of food and supplies. There are several different reasons why stores run out of items. The biggest of these reasons is called just in time logistics meaning stores maintain a smaller supply in the back to restock the shelves. This supply system offers the store numerous advantages, including fresher products and more floor space. However, if something happens to the supply chain, the store will not be able to restock and will quickly run out of products to sell.

As seen in California during 2019, weather issues are just one of the many things that can stop needed supplies from coming in. Other things that can cut off the supply system include truck drivers, warehouse workers, or others in the supply line going on strike, problems with suppliers, or problems with the road network or computer systems, all of which can lead to shortages.

This threat to the supply chain is just one reason to increase your food inventory, as well as other supplies on hand. Growing your supplies will prove useful in your everyday life, as well as you're preparing for disasters and any more significant events you may face. It will ensure that you don't have to run to the store for last-minute items if there is a run on the local store.

Man-Made Threats

Run, Hide, Fight

In 2018, there were 27 active shooter events in 16 states, including incidents at schools, concert venues, churches, and workplaces. During these incidents, there were 213 casualties, excluding the shooters, 85 people died, and 128 were wounded. These statistics point to prove that an active shooter incident can happen anywhere at any time. While you shouldn't live in fear, you and your family should have a plan to deal with such an event.

An active shooter is an individual that is attempting to kill and killing people in a confined and populated area. Usually, there is no reason why they chose their victims. Since these situations often are over 10 to 15 minutes, before law enforcement authorities arrive, it is crucial to ensure you are as mentally and physically prepared as possible to deal with defending yourself and loved ones from an active shooter situation and caring for those injured.

Action Recommendation:

The first step in preparing for an active shooter is to plan with your family, friends, and co-workers. Ensure everyone knows what actions they should take if confronted with an active shooter. Your plan should include the Run, Hide, and Fight Technique made famous by the US Department of Homeland Security. Anytime you enter a new building, you should identify the two nearest exits, and have an escape path in mind, as well as places to hide if need be.

Next, you should practice your plan. Your actions need to be muscle memory, and just like fire drills, it is important to rehearse the steps you will take during an active shooter situation.

If caught in an active shooter scenario, you should first try to **RUN** and escape if possible. Getting you and your group away from the threat should be a top priority. Leave your belongings behind and get your family and group to safety. Help others if you can without endangering yourself but evacuate the area and stop others from entering it. When you do get to safety, call 911, and describe the shooter, location, and weapons.

If you cannot run, **HIDE**. Get out of the shooter's view and stay very quiet, including silencing any electronic devices and turning off their ability to vibrate. Build a barrier between you and the shooter by locking and barricading doors, closing blinds, and turning off lights. Use text messaging to communicate with the police silently. You should look for both an area offering concealment, staying out of the shooter's view, and cover by ensuring you have something between you and the shooter that can block their bullets.

FIGHT if you need to. In doing so, you commit to this fight being life or death, either you or the shooter will most likely die, so fight like your life depends on it because it does. Use makeshift weapons like chairs, books, scissors, or anything else you have available and fight to kill.

There will be police from multiple agencies storming the area. You do not want the police to see you as a threat. Keep your hands visible and empty, and obey any commands they give. Understand that the police are there to end the event and will not stop to help the wounded. Follow the instructions and evacuate in the direction that the police tell you. Then after the situation is over, ensure the physical and mental wellbeing of your family. You just went through a lot and should not think twice about seeking help if you need it.

Civil Disorder

The United States has seen an increase in civil unrest during the last couple of years, and this can only be expected to increase in the future. Whether it's a protest or the reaction by the community after a large-scale disaster, quite often, there will be some level of civil unrest and some increase in crime within that area.

Action Recommendation:

So, if caught in a riot or protest that seems to be turning and you no longer feel safe, what should you do? If you do find yourself caught up in a protest or riot, first try to leave. If you can't go right away, keep to the edge of the crowd where it is safer. If you are caught up in the group, stay clear of glass shop fronts, stay on your feet, and move with the flow. At the first opportunity available, breakaway and seek refuge in a nearby building, or find a suitable doorway or alley and stay there until the crowd passes. When leaving the fringe of the demonstration, walk away, don't run as this will draw attention to you.

Try not to be identified as being one of the demonstrators by keeping well away from the leaders or agitators. If you were unable to leave the area and get arrested, do not resist. Go peacefully and contact your lawyer as soon as you are able. If you are out of the country and this happens, contact your embassy and travel insurance provider as soon as you can to help you resolve your predicament.

Electromagnetic Pulse (EMP)

While an Electromagnetic Pulse (EMP) is very similar to a solar flare in what it will do, there are some significant differences. First and foremost, it originates from within our atmosphere. An EMP, sometimes called a transient electromagnetic disturbance, is a short burst of electromagnetic energy. E.M.P. radiation causes rapid changes in the electrical and magnetic fields in an affected area, and this interference generally becomes disruptive or damaging to electronic equipment. At more intense energy levels, a powerful EMP can damage physical objects such as buildings and aircraft structures. In short, the EMP overloads the electrical grid in the area and ruins the items running off that grid.

Countries have been able to design weapons to deliver the damaging effects of EMPs. While the risk of terrorists getting their hands on one of these weapons might be remote, it is not impossible, and unfriendly nations do have these weapons. Should an EMP be set off at the correct altitude over the central United States, it may be able to wipe out much of the power grid of the United States.

Terrorism

On the morning of September 11, 2001, men, women, and children; fathers, mothers, brothers, sisters, sons, and daughters were working, playing, and enjoying their everyday life. Unfortunately, this all came to an end at 8:46 a.m. when American Airlines Flight 11 crashed through the North Tower of the World Trade Center, and the country stopped, changing forever. This change to our country happened when 19 Al-Queda terrorists hijacked four commercial airplanes, crashing the first two planes into the North and South towers of the World Trade Center and a third into the Pentagon.

When word about the other attacks reached the passengers of Flight 93, the first heroes of America's War on Terror, fought back, and the aircraft was crashed into an empty field in Pennsylvania 20 minutes by air from Washington,

DC, potentially saving the lives of numerous in the city.

The attacks claimed the lives of nearly 3,000 people from 93 nations: 2,753 people died in New York, 184 people at the Pentagon, and 40 people on Flight 93. The country was changed and soon to be involved in a war lasting over 18 years to date. The fact that 19 terrorists can change the world in the blink of an eye shows how fragile life is.

Terrorism works by spreading fear and chaos. Smaller but just as detrimental events occurring since September 11th may prove a better example. During the 2013 Boston Marathon, a blast from two homemade pressure-cooker bombs near the finish line killed three people and injured 180 others. The subsequent and unprecedented search for Dzhokhar ensued on April 19, with thousands of law enforcement officers searching a 20-block area of Watertown. Residents of Watertown and the surrounding communities were asked to stay indoors; the transportation system, most businesses, and public places closed, essentially bringing the city to a halt. Around 6:00 p.m., a Watertown resident discovered Dzhokhar hiding in a boat. Dzhokhar was shot and wounded by police before being taken into custody.

Unfortunately, the bombers were not the only individuals who were caught up in police activity after this event. On April 15th, several people near the scene of the blast were taken into custody and questioned, including one person police stopped walking away from the explosion; they detained him when some of his responses, in their words, made them uncomfortable. Law enforcement searched his Boston residence, and he was found to have no connection to the attack. One U.S. official stated, "he was just at the wrong place at the wrong time."

On the night of April 18th, two men riding in a taxi in the vicinity of the shootout were arrested and released shortly after that when police determined

that they were not involved in the Marathon attacks.
Another was arrested several blocks from the site
of the shootout with Dzhokhar and forced to strip
naked by police, fearing he might have concealed
explosives. The police released him after
determining he was an innocent bystander.

I'm not writing this to question any of the actions of
the law enforcement agencies during these events,
this is not the book to do that, instead to show how
these actions as well as locking down of the city
were a result of the fear that the bombers were
successfully able to bring to the city of Boston and
in a lesser sense the nation. Law Enforcement at
the time had no way of knowing who was involved,
and nobody knew if more bombings were possible.
This one event brought a community to its knees if
only for a short time.

Cyberterrorism

Terrorism isn't limited to violent, physical attacks. Cyberterrorism brings different threats, but potentially no less deadly affecting infrastructure and life support systems around the nation or globe.

As computers became more of a way of everyday life, so did cybercrime, cyber warfare, and cyberterrorism. There has been an increase in cybercrime starting in 2014 when a group known as the Guardians of Peace hacked Sony and then the potential that Russia hacked the 2016 elections. As these attacks become ever more frequent, it begins to show the threat that exists to not only U.S. national security, but also the infrastructure that we intensely depend on every day of our lives.

The truth of it is that most infrastructure control systems were built in the 1980s and 1990s when cyber threats, and therefore security, were not a concern that places our infrastructure in danger to such attacks.

Epidemics

We have all heard, watched on tv, and read the stories about the end of the world that was brought about by an epidemic. But in today's medically advanced society, what is the chance of an epidemic taking hold? During a Ted Talk Larry Brilliant, an American Epidemiologist discussed this and concluded that there would be a pandemic within our children's or grandchildren's lifetime.

The increased risk of an epidemic affecting our nation will be due to current activities that are expected to continue during the next few generations. First, we've dramatically increased our global population size. Secondly, we're moving to more central locations. Thirdly and possibly the most crucial, we can travel farther, faster, and more often, enabling the spread of germs around the world within a few days, if even that long.

In 2009, an influenza outbreak occurred, killing more than 18,000 people worldwide. Part of the identified problem with the spread was how rapidly the flu virus was able to spread and mutate.

Action Recommendation:

Though, there may be no perfect solution to prevent the spread of disease during an influenza outbreak, epidemic, or pandemic. There are, however, steps to help protect yourself and your family.

This begins with vaccines. While vaccines are becoming more and more controversial, they can act as a defense to the disease in the case of an outbreak. Once a vaccine becomes available, higher-risk individuals will be vaccinated first. If clinics begin mass vaccinations, be prepared to provide necessary medical information about your family.

In addition to vaccinations, take other necessary steps to stop the spread of disease:

Wash your hands with soap and water. Hygiene is crucial to staying healthy.

Avoid touching your nose, mouth, or eyes unless you've just washed your hands.

Cover your nose and mouth anytime you sneeze or cough. Wash your hands afterward.

Avoid crowds as much as you can.

Depending on the severity of the pandemic, wear a face mask if you go into a crowded area, or within 6 feet of others.

If you become infected:

Wear a face mask if you come into close contact with an infected person.

Stay home and away from people while contagious. This may be between 24 hours after your symptoms are gone and seven days after the onset of illness, whichever is longer.

If you need to seek care, call your healthcare provider before going to a clinic or the hospital. Let your provider know that you are coming in so they can make space away from the waiting room ready for you. If you have severe symptoms like difficulty breathing, you should seek immediate medical attention.

Wear a face mask anytime you need to go into a crowded area. If you don't have a face mask available, use a handkerchief. At a minimum, use a tissue when coughing or sneezing.

If possible, only have one person care for you and minimize contact with others.

If you exhibit any of the below symptoms, seek emergency medical care immediately:

Shortness in breath or Trouble breathing

Pain or pressure in your chest or abdomen

Dizziness or fainting

Confusion

Severe vomiting

Antiviral Medications

If available, prescription antiviral drugs can help with the treatment and prevention of influenza. They may come in a pill, liquid, or inhaled form.

Pandemic Preparation

Plan ahead in case service is disrupted, especially if someone in your family has special needs or requirements.

If possible, work from home.

Plan homeschool activities in case the school closes.

Stay as healthy as possible by getting adequate rest, managing your stress, eating right, and continuing to exercise.

Assist seniors in your community.

Build a sick room:

If possible, set up your Sick Room in a spare bedroom or other separate room. The area needs proper lighting, a window that opens, and access to a personal bathroom with a sink. If a separate room is not available, you will have to improvise by sectioning off part of an area in your home for the ill person. If the sick person and others have to use the same bathroom, all surfaces need to be cleaned daily with disinfectant (especially the sink and faucet handles). Towels, water bottles, drinking glasses, and other personal care items used by the sick person should not be used by other family members.

Conclusion

There are numerous threats out there, and this does not cover some of the more personal items that you should be preparing for, including financial, medical, or other personal issues, house fires, vehicle breakdowns, or vehicle accidents. If I were to include all the items that each person should be preparing for, I would have to write a different book for each reader. Instead, it is important to realize we live in an unpredictable world where weather, as well as human-made disasters, can happen at a moment's notice.

The following chapters will help you define the threats you are planning for and create a plan to deal with those threats.

Building Your Plan

Where to Begin

Governmental Disaster Plans

Each State, County, and most Cities have a Governmental Disaster Plan, and the best thing is they are a matter of public record. They will show us what the government in the area we live in sees as a threat, and what they plan to do during an emergency. We can take their plan and use it to create our own.

But where can we find these plans? At the minimum, each county has an emergency management department. They might be called an

Emergency Management Agency or an Office of Emergency Services depending on your state, but in most cases, they are a branch of the County Sheriff's office.

You can usually go online and search for your county's name along with the term "emergency management" to find the website. If that doesn't work, go to the county sheriff website and look there. If neither of these works, call the non-emergency business line for the sheriff's department and ask them how to contact the county's emergency management coordinator.

What's in the Plan

While the information may not be disaster-specific, the plans will give you an indication of how much, or how little, the government has thought about the various disasters likely to occur where you live. You can find this information in the risk assessment section of the plans helping you build your risk assessment.

Moving from there, you will find information on how the government plans to act at each point of the disaster.

Risk Assessment

The United States is a vast country, but it is nothing when you consider the diversity of the world. We do not all face the same risks or threats from disasters, either human-made or natural. The first aspect in determining many of the risk factors that you may face is determining the inherent dangers to where you live. By carefully evaluating your most significant risks, you can narrow your focus on specific threats. This narrowed focus will allow you to spend your time and resources preparing for the events that you have the highest odds of facing.

As you consider your risks, it is essential to keep in mind there are some hazards that you may have a reasonable amount of control over, others that you can show some influence over, and others that are entirely out of your control. It is important to spend your time, energy, and resources on what you can control or influence.

When preparing a risk assessment, I prefer using the Army's Composite Risk Assessment. A great source and one I decided to apply to this chapter, the United States Army FM 100-14, Risk Management, 23 April 1998. It is a proven method, quickly learned. Whether you decide to follow this one or a different method, it is crucial to ensure that you identify the hazards, assess the risks, develop controls, and make decisions to help you build your plan.

Preparing this risk assessment is a five-step process beginning with identifying the hazard to evaluating the effectiveness of your plan.

Step 1. Identify hazards. Consider your current situation, the environment, and known historical problems based on your location and past events. For instance, if you live in Northern California, you may be concerned with wildfires, but shouldn't worry about Hurricanes as Northern California does not regularly have to deal with Hurricanes. On the other hand, if you are currently working and not independently wealthy, you may place employment loss as an identifiable threat.

Step 2. Assess the risk to determine risk decisions. You need to find the impact of each hazard in terms of potential loss and cost based on probability and severity.

In assessing the risk, you will need to ask these questions:

What type of injury or damage can you expect from the threat?
What is the probability of the event happening?

Something expected to lead to minor injury combined with an unlikely chance equals a low-risk threat. An expected fatality or substantial loss connected with a frequent chance equals exceptionally high risk. For instance, in most cases, getting the flu during the year is extremely likely, but if you are otherwise healthy, it will not be a severe blow. However, your house catching on fire is less likely though possible, and extremely damaging. Therefore, your home catching fire is a higher risk than a healthy young adult catching the flu.

Step 3. Next, develop controls and make your risk decisions. If you cannot eliminate the risk, control it without sacrificing the essential elements of your life. Some risks can be controlled by modifying actions, changing locations, building backups, wearing protective clothing, changing the time of work, deciding to leave before the event, etc. As a leader in your family, you must choose between selecting from available controls, stopping where you are because the risk is too high, or accepting the risk because the benefits outweigh the potential losses.

Step 4. Implement control measures. Place controls to eliminate hazards or reduce their risks. Integrate procedures to manage risks into your plans and actions. Also, ensure you use the determined risk reduction measures when carrying out the project.

Step 5. Supervise and evaluate. Enforce standards and controls in your families; for the most part, this is being a caring parent or family member. Then evaluate the effectiveness of these controls and adjust or update them as needed. Make sure your family members know what controls are in place and what standards you expect, then hold everyone accountable for implementation from start to finish.

Below is a risk assessment form based on the DD 2977 used by the United States Army in preparing their risk assessments. I suggest using this when building your own as it is a proven tool used by the military and other organizations for years.

Task Description:					Date:
Risk Management: (1) Identify the hazards (2) Assess the hazards (3) Develop controls & make decisions (4) implement controls (5) Supervise and evaluate					
Subtask	Hazard	Initial Risk Level	Control	How to Implement	Residual Risk Level

Overall Residual Risk Level, with comments:

- € Extremely High
- € High
- € Medium
- € Low

Overall Plan and Recommended Course of Action

The below matrix is the one the Army uses; it is straightforward to use and will help identify your risk to a specific event. To use this threat matrix, decide the severity and probability of the risk, and this will tell you the risk level. For example, a 7.0 earthquake in the Bay Area of California is catastrophic, has happened, but happens seldom, making the quake a high-risk event. While this is an event that everyone in the Bay Area should plan for, it may not be the top event.

Risk Assessment Matrix

E = Extremely High Risk H = High Risk M = Moderate Risk L = Low Risk			PROBABILITY				
			Frequent	Likely	Occasional	Seldom	Unlikely
			A	B	C	D	E
S E V E R I T Y	CATASTROPHIC	I	E	E	H	H	M
	CRITICAL	II	E	H	H	M	L
	MARGINAL	III	H	M	M	L	L
	NEGLIGIBLE	IV	M	L	L	L	L

<u>Probability</u>:

Frequent – known to occur regularly

Likely – a common event

Occasional – Happens sporadically but not uncommon

Seldom – could happen at some time.

Unlikely – Can assume it will not happen, but not impossible.

<u>**Severity**</u>:

Catastrophic – May result in death or permanent total disability, significant property damage, or severe environmental damage.

Critical – May cause a temporary total disability or permanent partial disability. Significant damage to property or the environment. Security failure.

Marginal - Minor damage to equipment, possessions, or the environment. May result in injury or illness. Minor damage to property or environment may happen.

Negligible - Minor medical treatment may be needed. Slight equipment damage, but fully functional or serviceable. Little or no property or environmental damage.

United States Army FM 100-14, Risk Management, 23 April 1998.

Basics of

Emergency

Planning

Personalize your Emergency Plans to each individual or your family that the plan covers. However, there are a few general principles common to all. All emergency plans should include what to do if you need to leave or bug out, and what to do if you need to stay in place and ride out the event.

Needs buy-in from all involved - The plan should get buy-in from all involved. Include everyone who will be covered by the emergency plan in creating it. This way, you don't miss something important to someone in your family. Older children should be part of the conversation and listened to. They can lend a lot to the discussion from numerous different viewpoints.

Keep your plan organized and available- It needs to be a written plan that is available to anyone who needs it. Information that could be a security risk needs to be avoided or coded. I recommend giving each member a copy of your plan and having one in each vehicle. A prepping binder is an excellent tool for planning as well as keeping everything related to your emergency plan organized.

Writing Your Plan

After conducting your risk assessment, you can begin writing your emergency plan. Since your family may be separated when a disaster strikes, take into account that you may need to bring your family back together before or during your evacuation and include a plan to meet at a specific location or decide who will be picking who up. Know how you will contact others in your family during an emergency and establish a familiar and quickly found meeting place for your family if you are separated.

Put together a plan by discussing with your household, family, and friends how you will receive emergency alerts and warnings, what the shelter plan is, what are your evacuation locations (have at least three), what is the primary and secondary evacuation route is, and what is your communication plan.

<u>Shelter in Place or Bug Out:</u> Next, shelter in place or bug out. Choosing to take shelter is necessary for many emergencies, and being able to evacuate and ride out the storm at a loved one's home or a hotel may even be better. If you can, I always recommend leaving and getting your family or group to a safe location. Items can be replaced, loved ones cannot, and if you're not there, no one needs to worry about or rescue you. If the conditions make, it is necessary to shelter in place and stay off the roads and seek protection in your home, place of employment, or other safe location.

When deciding to shelter or evacuate, you need to consider what hazards you face then choose a place that is protected from that hazard or hazards.

Where you want to shelter will depend on the risks you are facing and the type of emergency.

<u>Bugging Out/Evacuating:</u> If you are going to bug out, everyone needs to know where you are going and how to get there. In planning your evacuation, you should identify several places in different locations and directions of travel that you could go to in an emergency. If you have pets, identify areas to stay that will accept pets and have the phone numbers and addresses for those locations in your plan.

Be familiar with possible alternate routes out of your area and understand that there may be a case where you must abandon your car. Therefore, I have bicycles for each member of my family ready to go if we must evacuate.

Assemble the supplies that you will need and have them ready for evacuation. You should have both a go-bag you can carry on you and supplies for traveling long distances in your vehicle. In your car, you should keep a full tank of gas and fuel it up if it gets down to a half of a tank. Gas stations may close during emergencies or unable to pump gas during a power outage. Have an emergency kit in the car. That kit should include the following:

A Car Kit

Jumper cables

Flares or reflective triangle

Ice scraper

Blanket

Maps

Cat litter for better tire traction if you get stuck

Wrench and socket set

Zip ties

Fluids for your car

Extra belts and hoses

Jack and spare tire

Fire extinguisher

Paper and pencil

Books and games

Water and food

Snacks

Flashlight with extra batteries

First Aid Kit

Dust masks and safety glasses

Car cell phone charger and external charger

Additional items for children or pets

If you have decided to evacuate, ensure that you take your emergency supply kit. You built it, and it would be horrible to find yourself without it now that you need it. That is why I recommend keeping your 72-hour or bug out bag (BOB) in your car when away from the house. It can be used for a lot of your travel needs and may be valuable for short stays at places in smaller family level emergencies also. Take your pets with you, but understand many public shelters may only allow service animals, and you will have to find specific accommodations for pets.

If time allows, you should call or email your out-of-state contact listed in your family communications plan. Let your emergency contact know you are safe, where you are going, what route you plan on taking, who you have with you and if you need to pick anyone up en route, time that you will contact them, and what to do if they don't hear from you.

Before you bug out, lock all of your doors and windows to make sure that you secure your home. Finally, leave a note telling others when you left and where you are going, this will help rescuers know that you are safe.

When you leave, wear sturdy shoes and clothing that provides some protection such as long pants, long-sleeved shirts, and a hat. The long sleeve shirts, boots, and pants will help protect you if you need to abandon your vehicle during the evacuation. If you have room, you may want to check with neighbors who may need a ride.

Finally, don't return to where you evacuated from until the "all clear" is given. First, you will likely not be able to return to the area until the evacuation is lifted. Secondly, the evacuated area is still dangerous.

Consider specific needs

As you write out your plan, ensure that you tailor your emergency plan to all those in your family or group. You should discuss your needs and responsibilities, and how people in your network can assist each other with everyday life. Your plan should include care of children, business needs, pets, and medical needs. Keep in mind the different ages of the members of your household, responsibilities for assisting others, dietary needs, medical needs, including prescription drugs and medical equipment, pets or service animals, and cultural and religious considerations.

Parts of Your Plan

I suggest performing a risk assessment, finding your more significant threats, deciding when to bug out and when to stay in place, then write a plan for each one using a military operations order style. Breaking your emergency plan into separate sections speaking about the Situation, Mission, Execution, Supplies needed, and the Communications Plan will help ensure you don't miss something.

Situation

The situation, based on your risk assessment, may begin with the most personal threats and work out to more significant ones that affect your area or work in the other direction. An example of situations may be as simple as your car has broken down, or it may be as large as you have received evacuation orders due to a category five hurricane or rapidly spreading wildland fire. The more situations you plan for, the more prepared you're going to be, but use the risk assessment to prioritize your planning.

Mission

The mission section is a general overview of what you are going to do. In the case of a broken-down car, this paragraph would include getting a replacement car for the time being and getting the car into the shop for repairs. For the evacuation, your task becomes to evacuate safely.

Execution

The execution describes the steps you will take to accomplish the mission. The execution section will include who will do what and when to accomplish specific items. It is easier to break this into phases. Example phases may be pre-disaster when you conduct your planning; warnings received when preparations need to get completed, emergency occurring, returning home, and recovery.

Supply

Your supply section should include what are you going to need for the situation, where you are going to get it, and who is responsible for ensuring the supplies are there. Supplies should include any bug out bags, car kits, as well as anything you will use if you decide to shelter in place. For more information, see the bug out and every day carry lists as well as the car kit list sections.

Communication

Communication is a crucial element of any plan. When people can't communicate, things begin to break down, leading to more panic. Therefore, it is essential to include a communications plan with your emergency plan. Realize that while we live in a world where we can routinely get on our cell phone and contact anyone in the world, in most cases during an emergency, your cell phone will not work.

Planning for a backup means of communication is crucial. For starters, each person in the family or disaster preparedness group should have a small laminated card with essential phone numbers. You should also utilize apps and websites that are currently available. For instance, your family or group should have a Facebook group where you can check-in, and others can monitor to see if you're alright or need help. I also like using Zillow to communicate with a group.

Your plan should follow P.A.C.E., which stands for Primary, Alternate, Contingency, and Emergency means of communication.

Primary: I recommend Cell Phones either using them to call or to text as your primary means of communication. Most people are comfortable with cell phones and use them every day; therefore, if available, it makes the most sensible solution.

Timed check-ins also need to be part of your written plans with agreed-upon actions to take if someone misses a scheduled check-in. Having this already determined will help set up a specific time interval for calls home or to other members of your group and helps prevent unnecessary worry on the part of those outside the affected area. Scheduling timed communication checks will also help you save the battery life on your phone; you can turn your phone off when not in use, knowing that family members know you won't be calling until your next check-in time.

If you can, instead of making a call, send a text as your text is more likely to make it through even when the cell phone towers become overwhelmed by everyone trying to call in and out. Text-messaging will also give you the ability to send a mass text.

***Alternate**: I recommend using radio communication as your alternate means, though it will only work for short-range communications.*

Radio Communications: There are, of course, many different types of radios on the market today. These range from those working on Family Radio Service (FRS) frequencies, General Mobile Radio Service (GMRS) frequencies, or dual modes that can transmit on either spectrum.

Radios generally work only with a line of sight communications, unless you can use a repeater, and only ranges a few miles at most.

Armature radio, commonly referred to as ham radio, is another option though it does require licensing. To obtain a license, you will have to take a test and pay a small fee, but HAM operators have a long history of assisting with communications during disasters.

Contingency: This may be using Facebook to leave posts that you are safe and as your messenger. I suggest creating a family group that can be semi-private but used by the family to stay in contact.

Emergency: This is your last chance of getting in contact and might include getting in touch with someone else to relay a message for you.

Prepping Binder and Thumb Drive

Binder

Your binder should be a three-ringed binder with divider tabs for each section. The different parts should include the following:

Emergency Contacts – This section is self-explanatory, but includes nearby relatives, poison control, hospitals, Red Cross, and any local disaster agencies you may have in your area.

Maps – This should include a topo and road map of your local area and the area you plan to go to. You should also have road maps of your state and surrounding states.

Bug-out information – Have information for hotels you may need to go to, and map of your bug out location with three routes to that location.

Financial Documents – Include addresses and phone numbers of all banks and credit card companies, essential documents related to employment or business, and copies of your insurance policies (life, health, auto, homeowners, other).

Personal Documents – This includes copies of your marriage certificate, birth certificates, driver licenses, CCW permits, pet vaccine records, passports, legal documents about child custody or adoption, and recent photos of each family member and each pet.

Medical Documents – Copy of health insurance cards, a list of blood types for each family member, doctors (names, addresses, and phone numbers), and a list of current prescriptions (dosage and pharmacy contact information)

Thumb Drive

Maps – This should include a topo and road map of your local area and any bug-out location you plan to use. You should also have road maps of your state and surrounding states.

Food and Water Storage – Containing ongoing inventory sheets to keep track of what you have on hand. It should also have recipes for quick and easy meals, and photos and descriptions of edible plants in your area.

For water, have information on how to disinfect water at home, and a list of possible sources of water nearby.

Financial Documents – Include copies of the fronts
and backs of debit and credit cards; copies of your
house and car titles; names, addresses, and phone
numbers of all banks; a copy of your will and/or
living trust; other vital documents related to
employment and/or a business; and copies of your
insurance policies (life, health, auto, homeowners,
other).

Personal Documents – Include copies of your
marriage certificate, birth certificates, legal
documents pertaining to child custody or adoption,
driver licenses, passports, social security cards,
CCW permits, a list of firearm serial numbers,
recent photos of each family member and each pet,
pet vaccine records, color photos of your house and
each room, pictures of anything of particular value,
military documents, diplomas and transcripts, and
appraisals.

Medical Documents – Copy of health insurance
cards, a list of blood types for each family member,

doctors (names, addresses, and phone numbers), medical history of each family member, immunization records, and a list of current prescriptions (to include dosage and pharmacy contact information)

Survival Gear – This section should include a checklist of what you have on hand and what you need to purchase. Also, include a list of your bug-out bag contents as well.

Bug-out information – Have information for hotels you may need to go to and a map of the area you plan to bug out to with three routes to that location marked.

Practice your Emergency Plans

Remember, Perfect Practice makes Perfect. It isn't enough to write your plans down, and then set them aside; you need to practice. Without practice, when confronted with that situation pushing us to fight or flight, we will freeze up if we don't know what to do. On the other hand, various studies show that if we practice our plan, it will become muscle memory, and we will react faster.

Doing drills and practice runs allows you to make mistakes, adjust, and move on with a better plan. Practice will cement the steps in your mind, allowing you to react quicker when under stress.

These drills can also serve to get others interested in preparing.

Drills can be planned, giving family members ample warning or as a surprise drill. A surprise drill will add more realism to the situation. I would ensure to include both in your training schedule. Start with planned exercises, and once everyone seems to be capturing the concepts, move to a surprise drill.

Sample Plans

Shelter in Place Plan

The first type of plan you should have is for sheltering in place at home. Since your home is where you spend most of your time, odds are the greatest that this is where you will be when an emergency hits. Fortunately, this is more than likely where you will have most of your supplies as well. With a quick tweak to this plan, you can change it to sheltering in place at work or school.

Situation

Anything from routine disasters such as winter storms and power outages to tornadoes and earthquakes and more may happen to force you to shelter in place. Even though FEMA now says to be ready to shelter in place for five days, my suggestion is to plan to provide for all of your own needs for a minimum of two weeks, since it is always better to be safe than sorry.

Mission

To provide a safe and secure place for your family to ride out the storm with as little disruption to their lives as necessary.

Execution

You will have to write this section based on your own needs, wants, and capabilities. Remember to account for everyone and assign needed tasks by name. Write a part for:

Before the Incident:
Include any planning, preparing, and work required to be ready to shelter in your home.

During the Incident:
What actions does your family need to take during the incident?

After the Incident:
What needs to happen to get you back to everyday life.

Tasks: Use this to assign specific tasks to each individual in your group.
Who:
When
What:

Why:

Supplies

You are going to have to ensure you can provide for your family's basic needs and keep them distracted during the emergency.

Your Supplies should include:
Food
Water
Medical or First Aid
Prescriptions
A way to keep them comfortable and safe
Entertainment

Communication

How will you communicate with your family? Remember to include your P.A.C.E. (Primary, Alternate, Contingency, and Emergency) plan and what to do if you can't reach someone during an

emergency.

Get Home Plan

If you are out, but your family is at home, or it would be safe for you to return home, you will want a plan to do so. This is also a plan that will have to be written for several separate situations. You will want one for work, school, or elsewhere, and one for each member of your family. Your plan to get your young child from school to home will be different than the high school teen, and these will be different than an adult from work because each has specific requirements, abilities, and limitations.

Situation

Plan for some or all of your journey will have to be completed without your car.

Mission

To get back to your family and your home.

Execution

You will have to write this section based on your own needs, wants, and capabilities. Remember to account for everyone and assign needed taskings by name. Write a part for:

Before the Incident:
Include any planning, preparing, and work required to be ready. This includes planning your route. With the likelihood of foot-travel in mind, the first step in making this plan is to sit down with a map and find several possible ways out. Keep in mind that a path may be blocked, so you will want alternates. After creating these route plans, make sure you travel them frequently to ensure you know the way. Identify landmarks that you can use to see that you are on the right path as road signs may not be present during the emergency. You should also

identify potential rest stops, and if possible, safe houses.

Assemble your get home bag. This may also be your bug out bag, but it is based on what you want. I use one bag for both, and it is available for other short trips. Your Get Home Bag should be able to sustain you during your journey home. See Supplies for a list of items for your get home bag.

During the Incident:
What actions to take during the incident.

After the Incident:
What needs to happen to get you back to everyday life.

Tasks: Use this to assign specific tasks to each individual in your group.
Who:
When
What:

Why:

<u>Supplies</u>

You are going to have to ensure you can provide for your family's basic needs and keep them distracted during the emergency.

Your Supplies should include:

Food and water: This should be enough to last you through your longest planned route on foot. This should be long-lasting, require no refrigeration, and minimal to no preparation before you can eat it. Think MREs, hiker meals, energy bars, jerky, and the like. Your water should not only include water attached to your bag, but methods to purify water while you move such as a sawyer filter or purification tabs.

Shelter / Warmth: Be sure to have at least one complete set of clothing and shoes for the walk if needed. A sleeping bag, blanket, or emergency blanket should also be carried.

Fire Starting Kit: This should start with a lighter, but can include strike anywhere matches, a Ferro rod, some tinder, steel wool, and a 9-volt battery, cotton squares, tinder sticks, petroleum jelly or Carmex lip balm.

Medical or First Aid: Include a small kit containing bandages, antibiotic ointment, burn cream, pain relievers, antacids, anti-diarrhea medications, elastic bandages for strains and sprains, tourniquet, and any medications you may take.

Security: These items are a judgment call on your part, and should be based on your own training and the applicable laws in your area. If you decide to carry a lethal weapon such as a firearm, make sure you do so legally. Whether you carry a gun or not, have some sort of less than lethal self-defense such as pepper spray or a taser.

Tools: A good knife should be a part of every survival kit. A multi-tool will also be handy. A Flashlight, compass, and map of the area may prove very useful.

Entertainment: Cards or something to keep people entertained during whatever downtime there is will work wonders in keeping morale up.

Communication

Have a planned way to communicate with your family on your way home. Remember to have a Primary, Alternate, Contingency, and Emergency plan.

Practice

Once you have your plan, practice it. If you plan to walk from work, then have a member of your family drop you off at work and walk home. Go for a hike with your bags as a family at least once a week, so you all get used to walking with the bags.

Getting the kids Home from School

Not only should you make plans for getting yourself home, but if you have school-aged children, there also must be a plan to get them back from school. This planning should start with talking to the school administrators about their disaster plans and policies on how to pick up your child from the school if there is an emergency. Obtain a copy of the school's crisis plan and any applicable policies in writing and place them into your own plan.

Once you understand the school's policy, start making your plan on how to get your child from the school. Identify who will pick your children up from school or daycare. My recommendation is that the parent closest to the school should be responsible for picking the children up. You might also think about adding a trusted family member or friend to the authorized pick up list at the school. Once you decide who is picking the child up, you need to determine where they will be taken.

Your children should be informed of your plans and kept up to date in regards to changes that may happen. A copy of the information your child will need during an emergency should be placed in your child's backpack, so they can review it if there is an emergency, this should also include a list of phone numbers that may be needed.

Evacuating from Home (Bugging Out)

The decision to leave home cannot be made lightly, but in many cases, it may be your best chance of remaining safe. As with anything else, there is a right way and a wrong way to bug out and heading for the hills without a plan will just make you another statistic.

As with sheltering in place, you need a plan. This plan will include when to bug out, where to go, how to get there, what to take, and who does what.

When to Bug Out

When to Bug Out is one of the most common questions that people in emergency preparedness, survivalist, or prepping ask. Unfortunately, this is also one of the most difficult to answer, as the answer is different for everyone based on their own circumstances and the event in question. You don't want to leave too early, yet you can't go so late you get stuck in the evacuation traffic or can no longer safely move. The actual scope of the disaster may not be easily determined right away. What at first may appear to be merely a small thing may turn out to be an enormous disaster quickly.

There are a few indicators that it's time to evacuate, though. The first of these being an evacuation order or potentially a warning being given. If the authorities are saying to evacuate the area, then it may be time to heed their advice and leave.

There are eyewitness accounts of looting from reliable sources. This must be eyewitness from a credible source, though, as, in the aftermath of a disaster, rumors run rampant. It is one thing to be told "I saw looting taking place," and a completely different thing for that same person to say, "I heard from some guy that their uncle heard from a friend that people were looting." When at all possible, you want to act on credible information rather than on rumors and stories.

Emergency Services are overwhelmed or unresponsive. I'm not making any accusations against the brave men and women that make up our emergency services, but significant disasters can quickly overwhelm available resources and capabilities. Our Emergency Service members are only human, and although they work very hard doing a challenging job, they can only work for so long before they are overtaxed. At some point, if the disaster gets too large, they will have to make a tough choice and realize they need to triage the scene so they can do the most good. When this happens, it's definitely time to go to a safer area.

If your gut tells you it's time to go. When it comes time to bug out or not, you need to trust your instincts. If you don't feel safe or think it's time to leave, then it is. You may only get one chance to go ahead of the disaster and the rest of those evacuating. You don't want to be sitting in traffic and find out that it's too late. Therefore, I recommend leaving early.

Where to Bug Out

Without a planned bug out location and route, bugging out means nothing. You are going somewhere, but you don't know where and therefore you don't know what direction to go in. Consequently, it is crucial to make your bug-out plan before you need it.

Ideally, you should have multiple locations available, each in a different direction, in case one route is cut off. If you plan to evacuate to a family member's home, make sure you speak to them beforehand, and if possible, leave some bedding and other supplies at their house in case you do have to evacuate there.

As you consider your options for bug-out locations, you need to consider the distance you will have to travel. Your site should not be so far that it's unlikely you will make it there, but it can't be so close that it will also be affected. On average, my recommendation is to find a place that is seventy to one hundred miles away. Any distance farther than that is going to be unrealistic to travel to.

In addition to distance, you will want to pick a location that is less populated but not remote. In the case of an emergency, a lot of people living in a city will evacuate to another city, adding to their current issues and taking a lot of lodging availability. A smaller town may be overlooked and might be a better place to go.

Once you know where you are going, take out a map and develop at least three routes to each location. This will help ensure that you can get there if one of the roads is blocked or closed.

Supplying your Bug Out Location

Once you select your bug out location, you need to stock it with supplies. Few of us can afford to have duplicates or triplicates of everything, but you want to have at least some supplies stocked at each bug out location.

At an absolute minimum, each location should have enough food and water for everyone who intends to shelter there. After you make an agreement with friends and/or relatives to use their homes as bug-out locations, put together a few boxes of survival supplies, including food, water, and bedding for them to store for you. You might also include a few sets of clothing for each family member, sleeping bags, toiletries, some cash, a credit card, and some other necessities.

Supplies

In writing a chapter on supplies for Emergency Preparation and overall Preparedness, I go back to a supply chain that I have used for the last 20 years, this being the Army Supply classes matched with a first in first out rotational method, for controlling your stock.

While I won't cover all the categories in this book, I will touch on class 1 (Food, Rations, and Water),2 (Clothing, individual equipment, tents, toolsets, maps, administrative, and housekeeping supplies),4 (Construction materials), and 8 (Medical equipment).

Class 1 Items (Food, Rations, Water)

Food Storage

During an emergency, your ability to obtain decent food is going to mark your ability to not only maintain the health of your family but their morale and spirits as well. After an emergency, there will be a run on the stores, and you don't want to have to rely on those stores or outside assistance to fill your family's stomachs.

Stocking up on food and rations before an emergency puts you in a position of control by giving you the ability to provide for your family on your own. While you most likely will not be able to serve a 5-course meal to your family, with what you have placed in storage, you can make sure your kids don't go to bed hungry and give them some sense of normalcy. The sign of success is when your young children go through an emergency and never even know they did. You can provide this through proper food storage and meal plan.

Your Refrigerator and Freezer

In the initial few days of an emergency leading to power outages, you will want to do a few things. First, ensure you give your freezer and refrigerator as much life as you can, and secondly, you will want to consume what you can from both before your food goes bad. If you don't take any actions to lengthen the life of your freezer, food will stay frozen for about twenty-four hours, provided you aren't opening the door that often. Your refrigerator will have even less time before items start going bad.

To begin, you need to buy and keep an appliance thermometer inside your refrigerator and freezer. According to the US Department of Agriculture (USDA), you should keep your refrigerator at or below a temperature of 40 °F and your freezer at or below 0 °F. By having a thermometer inside both your refrigerator and freezer, you will know when the temperature warms to an unsafe point.

A few additional actions to take to delay your food from spoiling include using an alternate power source to keep both your refrigerator and freezer running, freezing bottles of water, group your frozen food together in your freezer, and finally transfer items from your fridge to your freezer.

Using an Alternate Power Source

The first method of protecting food in your freezer and refrigerator should be to ensure that they keep running. This can be done by adding an alternate power source to the fridge and freezer in the form of a generator. Small generators can ensure that your appliance keeps running if you have a power outage. To ensure that you maintain the safety and health of your family, never run your generator in your house or garage. Place your generator minimum of 15 feet from your house and point the exhaust away from your home and any windows, doors, or vents.

Frozen Bottles of Water and Ice

Keep frozen water bottles in your freezer. The more space there is in your freezer, the quicker items will thaw out and eventually spoil. By placing water bottles in your freezer, you will take up this open space. You can also use these if you must transfer your food into a cooler. Not only will this keep frozen food cold longer, but you can count this towards your supply of fresh drinking water.

Another step to take is to empty your ice cubes into a gallon-sized storage bag each time the tray becomes full. You can then use the bags of ice to keep the coolers cold.

Group Frozen Food in the Freezer

Group your food together in the freezer. This helps the food stay cold longer for the same reason listed above; the more space there is in your freezer, the quicker items will thaw out and eventually spoil.

Move Items from your Refrigerator to your Freezer

If you have advance notice that there is a possibility of a power outage, you should transfer some of your refrigerated food to your freezer to keep it at a safe temperature for a more extended period. Items such as milk, meat, and leftovers can be placed in your freezer.

Eat the food from your Refrigerator first

Don't begin by eating your prepper food or shelf-stable food. To ensure that you don't waste food, you should start eating the food in your fridge, followed by your freezer. If you follow the above suggestions, you should be able to keep your food at a proper temperature without most of it spoiling before you can eat it. After you've consumed fresh, refrigerated, and frozen food, or it is no longer safe to eat, you will need to turn to your shelf-stable foods.

Shelf Stable Food

It is crucial to maintain a supply of shelf-stable food. This is the food that you will turn to after your fresh and cold foods have been consumed or food that you will use to supplement those foods to ensure your family has enough to eat. While ready.gov recommends having a three day supply, I suggest you have a minimum of two weeks to begin with, and then build your pantry from there. My current goal is three months' worth of shelf-stable food.

Planning your Pantry

When planning your pantry, you should choose foods your family will eat, remember any dietary needs that exist, and avoid foods that will make you thirsty.

 Your pantry should be part of your everyday life, and the food in it should be stuff that you already eat. There is no point in storing food for an emergency, never to be eaten. Instead, you should build upon the food that you already eat and increase its supplies. This will ensure you continue feeding your family through the crisis. This also allows you to know that you have food for dinner without having to run to the store, even if your teenager brings some friends over unexpectedly. Have a food plan for your pets as well.

Pantry Rotation

Since you are storing food that you already eat for your long-term storage, it is crucial to use a first in first out method of inventory. This is done by facing your pantry, just as if it were a retail store. When I say facing, I mean organizing your pantry by the item pulling older items to the front, and placing newer items in the back. By rotating and facing your food, you will ensure that you don't end up with outdated food.

Suggested Emergency Food Supplies

No-Cook Foods: Start with foods that you can just open and eat with no preparation. Items such as beef jerky, granola bars, trail mix, peanut butter and crackers, and seeds will go a long way and make things easy. They are also great for road trips, hiking, and any time you need to grab something and go. Don't overlook the essential comfort foods, either. Cookies, chips, a couple of cans of soda, and some other snacks can make a scary event into something fun for the kids. One night of junk food isn't going to hurt anything under these circumstances.

Boil and Eat: Canned foods and pasta fit in this category. This is something that you can just open and warm-up without a whole lot of preparation. Also, keep in mind that soup and stew can be a comfort food that everyone will enjoy with a little bread or crackers, and you can always spice it up with a few herbs and a little seasoning. This also includes many dehydrated foods and vegetables. Don't forget a couple of manual can openers. If you have canned food but only an electric can opener, you may be panicking.

Just add water mixes: Avoid mixes that require the use of milk, eggs, and other ingredients. You can get around this if you plan beforehand, and include dried milk and powdered eggs into the mix and repackage. This is the stuff you will begin using if the emergency lasts longer than a couple days. Included with these are pancakes in the morning, some cakes and cookies, bread mixes, and similar items.

BBQ items: Just because the power goes out, doesn't mean you have to suffer. If you can go outside during the emergency, it is crucial to have a BBQ that you can cook on and extra fuel. If you cannot go out, stick with the other items. Under no circumstances should you bring your BBQ grill indoors. This could lead to asphyxiation.

Beverages: Don't forget to add things like drink mixes, tea bags, instant coffee, and other stuff you drink; yes, even soda if you drink it.

Gardening

The best way to keep produce fresh is to keep them growing in your garden. Based on where you live, there are things you can do to have a garden year-round. Whether it's just a couple of plants inside your apartment or a large garden through most of the year in your backyard. Replacing shrubs with fruit-producing trees and bushes is also recommended.

Obtaining the Food to Build your Pantry

To be completely honest, to get enough food for your family is going to cost some money. Most of us don't even have one week of food in our house, not to mention two or more. So instead of buying all the food at once, add to your storage a little each time you go to the store. Next time you need a can of peas, grab two or three. If you get a box of mix, grab another. A couple of extra items each week will add up quickly, and before you know it, you will have a decent pantry.

Shop the sales ads and use coupons when you can.

Food Safety and Sanitation

When planning your emergency meal preparation, you must also consider food handling protection requirements. The risk of foodborne illness is higher while handling raw food. You need to ensure proper handwashing techniques are observed and ensure that dishes, utensils, and other items used with food are adequately cleaned.

Bacteria in food will proliferate at temperatures ranging between 40 and 140 °F, and if these foods are consumed, you can place yourself at risk from becoming violently ill. Thawed food can usually, but not always, be eaten if it is still below 40 °F but to be safe: if there is doubt, throw the food out.

To further protect yourself from getting sick due to food safety, ensure that you keep food in covered containers and discard any food that touches contaminates, has been at room temperature for two or more hours, has an unusual odor, color, or texture.
Never from cans that are swollen or corroded, even if the food looks safe to eat. Never eat food that looks or smells abnormal.

Cooking

Numerous alternative cooking sources can be used in times of emergency. These include chafing dishes, fondue pots, fireplaces, outdoor grills, camp stoves, Dutch ovens, patio fire pits, backpacking stoves, and numerous other methods. Keeping in mind that many of these are for outdoor use only. Commercially canned food may also be eaten out of the can without even warming it. If you do want to cook it, though, you can heat it right in the can. Simply remove the label, thoroughly wash the can, then just open and heat it up.

Chafing dishes and fondue pots: These should go without explanation, as the purpose behind these is to warm up and keep food warm for long events.

Fireplaces: These used to be the go-to when cooking for the family, and if you have the proper cookware, these can become a ready substitute for any oven.

Outdoor Grill: This also seems obvious enough, but don't underestimate this backyard favorite. In addition to grilling, most newer grills have burners and other features that make cooking a breeze. It is a complete outdoor kitchen. For most people, this will probably be their first method of cooking until the propane or charcoal runs out. Make sure you store extra fuel.

Camp Stoves: This classic has never let me down. Easy to prepare multiple meals with the two burners. These cook like any stovetop while allowing you to cook without electricity while keeping the heat outside, helping you keep your home cool. Between this and my outdoor grill, I'm trying to cook outside more during the summer to keep the temperature inside the house down.

Dutch Ovens: Simple and classic, just build a fire and use either a stick or rocks to hold the Dutch oven or place directly over the coals. Dutch ovens are a must-have, you can use it outside or in your fireplace.

Patio Fire Pits: These popular favorites can currently be found in most backyards and used as an alternate cooking source by adding an old grill gate and using it similarly to a charcoal grill.

Backpacking Stoves: These small single burners attach directly to a fuel canister, and are easy to assemble and cook with.

Rations

Whether it's Military MREs, Augason Farms, Mountain House, or some other brand of food you can find in the camping section of your big box store, you should keep a brand that you like on hand. Try a few because you will find that you enjoy some meals from each brand better than other brands. Most of these just need the addition of either hot water or water into a heater packet to cook them. Once again, you must find one that you like because they are not all made the same, and some taste better than others.

Conclusion:

Assembling a food storage system including shelf-stable food and rations may seem daunting, but by building it a piece at a time and choosing a method to cook your meal, you can keep your family fed and moving.

Emergency Water

The importance of having clean water during and after an emergency cannot be overemphasized. Waterborne illnesses are one of the top causes of death around the world. Any person engaging in heavy exertion will need more water than they usually would on a regular day. Dehydration can kill, and although the often-quoted rule of thumb is that you can survive three days without water, it does not take into account that the majority of people usually don't drink enough water, to begin with, and drink more diuretics than water, dehydrating themselves on an everyday basis.

Your plan should also include being able to find additional water and having methods to purify it.

How Much:

So how much water should you keep on hand? The Centers for Disease Control and Prevention says, "the general rule of thumb is to store one gallon of water per person each day." They also suggest that, in an emergency, you drink two quarts (half a gallon) of water a day – more if you're in a hot climate, sick, pregnant, or a child. The problem with this is you have no idea how long the emergency is going to last. Secondly, one gallon of water a day is not enough to really keep you hydrated and account for other uses of water, including food preparation and hygiene.

I suggest a minimum of 2 gallons of water per person per day for a full week or 14 gallons per person due to these reasons. This will give you a cushion to fall back on if you need it because the event lasted longer than you had planned, or you use more water than expected. If you have pets, you will need to account for them as well. Plan a gallon a day per pet.

Storage:
Now that we discussed how much water you need, how are you going to store it? Start with making sure you are using your store and replacing it so that you don't have water sitting for years. FEMA recommends that the water should be rotated out about every six months.

There are several different water storage containers on the market today, ranging from small plastic bottles to 50-gallon barrels. Since you will likely have to move these at some point, you will want something that you can work with. For most, this means that the 5 gallon or 7-gallon sizes will be as heavy as they can manage. This may be a water cooler bottle or a water brick. I like using water cooler bottles because I have a water cooler in my house, but I like the idea of the water brick because they are stackable and easy to store. Each has its own advantages and disadvantages.

Another storage option is the WaterBOB, which is basically a large plastic bag that you place into your bathtub and fill it from the bathtub faucet.

Obviously, this isn't something you'd keep filled just in case, but rather a device you'd utilize when the disaster hits or warnings are being given. The WaterBOB will hold up to 100 gallons of water and will keep it fresh for up to four months. Keep in mind that if a boil water warning is given, you will still want to boil the water in your WaterBOB, but having water that needs to be treated is better than not having water.

There are also Vertical water tanks. These above-ground tanks are ideal for storing drinking water, harvesting and collecting rainwater, and as an emergency water supply.

Whether you buy individual containers, cases of water, or use recycled bottles, once you decide how to store your water, you need to choose where to keep it. Store the water in a cool, dark place. Basements work well, but if you don't have a basement, all is not lost. Use the space under your bed or couch, the floor in the back closet, or in the back of your kitchen cabinets.

Where to find additional water:

In the Home:
Even if you go through your water stores, you can find water inside your home. The first of these places to find water is your hot water heater. The

average hot water heater holds forty to fifty gallons of water. You can get to that water by draining your water heater. A second potential source of water in your home is the toilet tank, though if you routinely add any sort of cleansers to the tank, the water in the tank cannot easily be made potable.

To drain the water heater:

Step 1

Locate the water heater circuit breaker in the home's electrical panel and turn it off. If you are unsure of the correct circuit-breaker, turn the home's main power breaker off.

If you own a gas water heater, turn the gas supply valve off, and the gas control valve switch to the "pilot" setting.

Step 2

Turn off the water supply valve located on one of the two copper pipes coming out of the water heaters top by turning it clockwise.

Step 3

Connect a garden hose to the tank drain valve located on the bottom side of the tank. Some water heater drain valves resemble a standard water spigot, while others employ a plastic fitting.

Step 4

Run the hose to your storage container. Ideally, the drainage-end of the hose should be lower than the bottom of the tank allowing gravity to aid in the drainage process. If gravity can not be used, attach a manual hose siphon pump to the drain end of the hose.

Step 5

Next, flip the pressure-relief valve up to open it. This valve is attached to a copper pipe along the side of the tank. If the valve is kept closed, a vacuum may form inside the tank, slowing water flow.

Turn the drain valve counterclockwise and check the hose to ensure the water is running. If the water is not running or is flowing too slowly, follow the manufacturers' instructions to manipulate the siphon pump.

What Will You Need

Garden hose
Manual garden hose siphon pump (optional)

Tips

Monitor the water flow and the drainage area every few minutes to ensure a continuous steady stream and prevent water build-up in your drainage area.

Never drain a hot water heater while hot water is present, or the heater is operating. Doing so can lead to severe injury. Water temperature could be at safe levels after electricity or gas has been shut off after several hours.

Outside the Home:

Outside your home, several potential sources of water can be considered. These include rain barrels, collecting dew, streams, or melting snow if available.

Rain barrels are great if you live in a house. Simply install a fifty-five-gallon drum to the downspouts on your gutters to collect the water. Even a moderate rainfall collecting in this system will fill the barrel. If you can, daisy chain a couple of barrels together using kits that you can find in any home improvement store.

Purifying Water:

Once you have consumed all your water, if you dont replenish it, you may become dehydrated leading to more severe medical issues such as heat exhaustion or heat stroke. Dehydration can be prevented, though. Water purification removes undesirable chemicals, biological contaminants, suspended solids, and gases from the water, producing water fit for consumption.

Nowadays, it has become effortless to purify water. You can clean water by treating it with a chemical, either chlorine or iodine, using a filter or ultraviolet light, or boiling the water. All these methods are effective, provided they are correctly done. You only need to choose one way that you are comfortable with.

Boiling

Boiling is a very reliable way to purify water. Keep in mind that boiling uses fuel and takes time. You will need to use a cloth or other filter to remove any solid particles in the water you've collected, especially if the water was taken from a doubtful water source before boiling it. The biggest issue is, on summer days, it is not actually appealing to drink hot water.

Use of Iodine solution, tablets, or crystals

While, the use of Iodine solution, tablets, or crystals is an effective and more convenient method than boiling. It takes thirty minutes before you can drink the treated water, is not suitable for pregnant women, and has an aftertaste that you might not like.

To use, drop the tablet into the water container, shake the container and hold the bottle upside down with the lid slightly unscrewed, allowing the iodine to flow into the threads of the bottle cap.

Use chlorine drops

Chlorine is a lightweight, affordable, and easily accessible method to kill bacteria in water. You will need to wait for about thirty minutes before you can drink the treated water. You need to make sure not to put so many drops, as it could also be poisonous if used too much.

Use water filter

Water filters can remove bacteria in water. Carbon, on the other hand, gets rid of the chemicals and awful tastes while iodine coated screens can further remove viruses. Treated water can be consumed after the treatment, and the water should not have any bad taste. However, filters are heavier than iodine or chlorine and more costly.

Conclusion:

Since water can become limited, it is crucial to reserve your stored water and any water you disinfect for consumption. Do all you can to ensure you have a good supply of potable water during your emergency.

Class 2 Items (Clothing, individual equipment, tents, toolsets and kits, hand tools, maps, administrative and housekeeping supplies, and equipment)

This category covers most of the items that make up your kits and your bug out bag. Remember that your bug out bag can also be used for your bug-in bag and numerous other events to include going somewhere for a few days. While discussing your Class 2 items, I will be discussing the bags and kits.

Your Get Home Bag

Your Get Home Bag is similar but different from your bug out bag. While the bug out bag is designed to get you from home to a safe location and sustain you for the time you have to evacuate, the get-home bag is intended to include the things that you need to get home and back to your family.

For this reason, the get home bag is smaller and lighter than the bug out bag. Though many decide to use their bug-out bag as their get-home bag as well, to consolidate their bags. If you cannot carry your bug-out-bag with you, you should have a get home bag as a minimum. If you do have a separate get home bag, you will see some duplication between the two bags and the workplace emergency kit as well. Personally, my get home bag is in an assault pack that I can attach to my bug out bag when I have both or detach if I can only carry the get home bag.

Your get-home bag should contain the following:

1.   Complete Change of Clothes
2.   Food and Water
3.   First Aid Kit
4.   Fire Starter Kit with tinder
5.   Emergency Shelter
6.   Multi-Tool
7.   550 Cord
8.   External Battery and Cord for your Phone
9.   Flashlight
10.   Work Gloves
11.   Dust Mask
12.   Sunglasses and Clear Safety Glasses
13.   Street Map and Compass (Route Maps)
14.   Comfort items
15.   Self Defense Tools

Complete Change of Clothes: This one depends on your local climate and the time of year, but the clothing that you pack should be durable and comfortable for walking. In the winter, I add a stocking cap and gloves to my get home bag and use them when needed. I also recommend adding a poncho and jacket. Getting wet in cold temperatures can quickly turn into hypothermia. It's better to stash a poncho or jacket with a hood and not worry about walking in wet clothes in frigid temps. I also keep a fresh pair of socks and a pair of shoes. I keep shoes or hiking boots that I have just replaced as my spare pair. They are still in decent condition, but not what I want to wear every day any longer.

Hand and foot warmers are also a good idea when it's cooler.

Food and Water: Pack enough food and water for your journey, plus a little extra. Keep in mind that you won't need complete meals or days worth of rations. You simply need something small to tide you over and give you a little energy. Some protein bars and trail mix will work for your get-home-bag.

I also carry a steel bottle filled with water, and yes, I take some energy drink powder to put in it too. So why steel? You don't want plastic, or double-walled, neither works if you need to boil water. Plastic bottles will melt, and double-walled insulation makes it challenging to transfer enough heat to the water to get it to a boil.

You will also want several methods to purify and filter any water you might need to grab while on the move. I recommend packing an inline water filter and water purification tablets. I personally carry a sawyer mini water filter. Not only is it small and easy to pack, but it can also filter 100,000 gallons of water.

First Aid Kit: Start with a tourniquet and include items such as adhesive bandages, antibiotic ointment, moleskin, pain relievers, and other personal medications.

Fire-Starter Kit with tinder: It's impossible to know all the different ways a fire might come in handy in a survival situation. Your fire-starter kit should include lighters, strike-anywhere matches, fire steel, and tinder. You never want to depend on your lighter alone it may get wet, crushed, or damaged in another way. Therefore, you also need strike-anywhere matches. Once you have your items to start a fire, you still may have issues. No matter how experienced you may be under the wrong conditions, it can be surprisingly difficult to start a fire. To be successful, begin with a fine ignitable tinder (I recommend petroleum jelly soaked cotton balls)working your way to kindling and then full-sized logs. If you know you have a dry tinder with you, it makes starting the fire all that much easier.

Emergency Shelter: You can't always assume you'll make it back home driving, or in only a few hours of walking, it might take several days. So, it is wise to pack a lightweight shelter option for frigid overnight temperatures.

Multi-Tool: You should always pack a good quality multi-tool. Many people state you should pack both a knife and a multi-tool, and while I do, I also don't see this as a hard-fast rule as you should have a knife blade on your multi-tool.

550 Paracord: The number of uses for paracord is vast and limitless. So, always make sure you have paracord with you. You may choose to wear a bracelet or just roll it up in your bag.

External Battery and Cord for your phone: If your phone dies, you lose so much: communication, navigation, new reports, and more, therefore, it is crucial to always maintain a charged external battery and extra charging cable for your phone.

Flashlight: You should always have the ability to produce light. First, not all disasters happen in the middle of the day, and emergencies often include power outages. Secondly, even under normal circumstances, you never know when you need to look for something in a dark area. Therefore, it is crucial to carry a flashlight, and I recommend having a headlamp. With a headlamp, you can work with both hands while you hold your own light, putting it exactly where you are looking.

Work Gloves, Dust Mask, and Sunglasses clear safety glasses and more: Never overlook the importance of personal protective equipment. Your personal protective equipment should include gloves to protect your hands, glasses to protect your eyes, a dust mask safeguarding your lungs, earplugs or other hearing protection, closed-toe shoes or hiking boots, and a long sleeve shirt or light jacket. Given that you could be moving through areas that may be filled with storm damage and other debris, these could prove vital.

Street Map and Compass (Route Maps): Pack a street map and a compass, so you don't lose your way. I also recommend printing routes from google maps to save you time in developing your course. Remember, a map is great, but if you want to successfully navigate in unfamiliar areas, you'll also want a compass.
I'd rather have a compass and not need it than need it and not have one.

Comfort items: These are the items that you are willing to carry to make things more comfortable for you.

Self Defense Tools: This might be lethal or less than lethal weapons. It could be anything from a handgun, to pepper spray, to a taser depending on what you are comfortable and legally able to carry. Even if you do always carry a firearm concealed on you, I recommend also having something less than lethal, giving yourself more options of force if you need to defend yourself.

Bug-Out Bags

This is an area that needs quite a bit more time to speak about. From the type of pack to what is in it will make all the difference. The bugout bag is designed to provide all your basic needs until you reach a safe location and then continue supporting you after you reach that location. It is essential to inspect the contents regularly and, if possible, always keep it with you. If you have a car when you are driving the vehicle, it needs to be in the trunk if possible. This will eliminate your need for a get home bag. Your bug-out bag can quickly become your bug in and get home bag as well.

Most survival books plan a bug out bag for in the field survival. While this may be important, it is also just as important to plan your bag to get you through any event that you may face. This might be backcountry survival, but it is more likely going to be a scenario where you have to pick up and go help someone for a day or two, visit someone in the hospital, or something else where you have to stay somewhere unexpected for a couple of days. So include this in your thinking when planning your bag.

Generic contents of your bug out bag should include:

1.	Shelter and bedding
		Tarp
		Tent
		Sleeping bag

Pillow
Air Mattress

2.   Clothing (Season Appropriate) with a
                Waterproof nylon rain jacket
                Knit watch cap
                Baseball cap
                Warm gloves
                3 days of clothing
                Towel
                Flip flops
                Spare shoes
                Night eye mask
                sewing kit
3.   Hand and foot warmers
4.   Fire Making Kit
5.   Food and Water
6.   Medical Kit/First Aid Kit
7.   Hygiene Items
8.   Tools
9.   Navigation Items
10.   Lighting
11.   Security Items
12.   Comfort Items
13.   Bug out binder and thumb drive

Shelter: Depending on what you want to carry and what you have, this might be a backpacker's tent or a waterproof tarp and some cordage. I personally have a modular bug out bag and have a tent with my 72-hour bag, and a poncho and cord in my get home bag that connects to the front.

Fire Making Kit: I know, I just said that you should not build your bag to be a tactical ninja living in the backcountry, instead to make it for real-life situations, and then I go right to a fire-making kit. The bottom line is this kit will not only come in handy to keep warm camping or backpacking but also if you are in your backyard bbq, asked to start a fire in a fireplace or in a fire pit. You should keep multiple ways of starting a fire. To do this, you should build a fire-making kit. Making your own fire starter kit can be fun, and you will know everything in the package. In making this kit, it is crucial not to rely on only one method to get your fire lit. Many experts recommend having up to five fire starting options.

Container: To build your kit, you will want a watertight container to hold everything. This can either be a box or a small dry bag, I recommend the small dry bag. Next, what to put in the bag, let's start with the most straightforward item to start a fire with: a lighter.

Lighter: For many fire lighting situations, a lighter will get the job done. But they can become useless based on numerous factors to include fuel running out, in the rain or wind, and they can break.

Also, in icy conditions, the butane can become gel-like, causing the lighter to fail. So, you'll need a backup.

Waterproof Matches: waterproof matches are a must-have, they will work well when the conditions are right. Even though they say waterproof for extra protection, store them in a watertight container, and never rely on them solely.

Fire Stick: These are very convenient and reliable to get a fire started, and a great third option after the lighter and matches has failed. They are usually a magnesium alloy that can be scraped or used with a striker to create sparks.

Candles: candles are great to light and drip wax onto your tinder, act as a constant flame to start the kindling on fire. They are also a good backup light source if your batteries run down.

Cotton and petroleum jelly: Cotton dipped in petroleum jelly is a superb, cheap, and lightweight DIY fire starter. It's also easy to just grab a few bits at home to replenish your fire starter kit after use. You can also use Carmex instead of petroleum jelly.

Tinder: Cotton balls, dry grass, Cattail fluff, Birch tree bark, and Dandelion clock all make great tinder.

Food: We spoke in length about food earlier in this book, but for your bug-out bag, you will want three full days of food at a minimum. Stick with the food items that are shelf-stable and require no food preparation. Also, look for lighter meals, so stay away from canned foods. Great choices include:

1.	Jerky
2.	Granola or protein bars
3.	Trail Mix
4.	Nuts
5.	Peanut butter snack packs
6.	Crackers
7.	Ramen Noodles
8.	MREs or other Rations
9.	Other similar foods

Also having:
1.	Eating utensils
2.	Can opener
3.	Bottle opener
4.	Mess kit

Water: Plan to carry some water with you but also have the means to filter and disinfect more water as you go. Have:

1.	A minimum of 2 liters of water
2.	Water purification tablets
3.	Portable Water Filtration System

Medical First Aid: This will be discussed in Class 8 (Medical Supplies). Just keep in mind that you are not going to have space for a full-blown trauma kit in your bug out bag. You will, however, need items to take care of injuries and some of the more common ailments that are going to be faced during a bug-out situation. Avoid liquid medications, since they might leak after being bumped around in the bag.

Hygiene: By having a few hygiene items, you can help keep your morale up while staving off potential infections and illnesses by keeping clean. Items I suggest having on hand include:

1.	2-3 washcloths or hand towels (Wysi Wipe, Hypoallergenic Reusable Wipes Singles For Cleansing Baby, Hands, Face, 100-pack, Just Add Water) these are great they are pill size to begin and expand in water.
2.	Travel size container of liquid soap
3.	Hand sanitizer
4.	Travel size toothpaste and toothbrush
5.	Dental floss
6.	Toilet paper (remove the center tube to crush down

7.   Baby Wipes (Wysi Wipe, Hypoallergenic
Reusable Wipes Singles For Cleansing Baby,
Hands, Face, 100-pack, Just Add Water)
8.   Feminine supplies and personal hygiene
items

Tools: By adding just a few tools to your bag, you
can increase your odds during an emergency.
These will add weight to your kit but will ensure you
have the tool you need when you need it.

1.   A good quality fixed blade knife
2.   Multi-tool
3.   Box cutter
4.   Small pry bar
5.   Contractor-grade garbage bags (several)
6.   Duct tape
7.   Paracord
8.   Small notebook and pencil
9.   Personal Protective Equipment (gloves,
safety glasses, and a dust mask)
10.   Plastic ties
11.   Wrench or pliers to turn off utilities
12.   Mini shovel
13.   Hatchet
14.   Wire or folding saw

Navigation: To get to your bug-out location or even
just home during a crisis, you need to have a way
to figure out which way to go if you have altered

your course. While you should have a good GPS program on your phone, you also need to have alternate methods to navigate your route. Your navigation tools should include the following:

1.   **Cell phone with GPS software:** A good GPS program should already be programmed onto your phone. I use google maps, this program not only allows you to navigate your route, but you can also save offline maps on your phone. I recommend having a copy of your top 3 ways to your primary and secondary evacuation or bug-out locations. Using google maps, if you have data, the members of your family or group can share their positions with each other to help ensure that everyone can be recovered before bugging out.

2.   **Maps and compasses:** Have maps of the area, including routes, street level, and topographical for the surrounding areas. I keep street maps of the town I live in and work in, the counties, and the state.

3.   **Google map directions:** You should have printed out copies of your evacuation routes with marked rally points in your bug out binders.

Lighting: Lighting is crucial. It keeps your family comfortable, allows you to navigate from sundown to sunrise, and maintain your security:

1.   **Headlamp:** A headlamp will give you a hands-free option enabling you to work with both sides while having light available. A good headlamp should be your first choice as a light source.

2.   **Flashlight:** Everyone knows the importance of a good flashlight. This should be more powerful than your headlamp.

3.   **Chem Lights:** These can be very useful in lighting an area and can be fun for the kids. You can change the mood of the situation by giving a couple of chem-lights to your kids.

4.   **Camp lantern:** This is an excellent option for families. This will allow you to be in a lighted space without having to have all the flashlights on facing each other.

Security Items: The items you have security is a personal decision. Not everyone feels safe with a firearm, wants to carry one, or can legally in their area. If you don't feel safe doing so or can't legally have a gun with you, do not carry one. There are plenty of other options. If you can and do decide to take a gun, you should do so safely. This means that you need to get training and practice with your weapon. Along with carrying the gun which should stay on your person at all times, you should also pack the following supplies:

1.   100 rounds of ammunition
2.   Cleaning kit
3.   Gunlock
4.   CCW Insurance (highly recommend being covered by USCCA, NRA, or another insurance plan if you have a gun)

Whether you decide to carry a firearm or not, you should also have the means to defend yourself that is less than lethal. Once again, check your local and state laws to ensure you comply with the current laws and are legally protected. Options for this are not limited to but can include:

1.   Pepper Spray
2.   Stun gun or Taser
3.   Expandable batons
4.   Large Flashlight
5.   You may also think outside the box

Comfort Items: There are a few items that, while not life-sustaining, are still crucial for the well being of yourself and your group. These include things to keep your family entertained, such as:

1.   Puzzles and games

2.   Deck of cards
3.   Books
4.   Video games
5.   Audiobooks
6.   Additional external batteries for cell phones
7.   Power strip and extension cords
8.   Candies and snacks

Vehicle Kit

If you own a vehicle, you should have an emergency kit in your trunk. This will help you if you need it or may make you the hero by helping someone else out someday. Your vehicle kit should cover the needs of your vehicle and your passengers. Feel free to add to it as you see fit and consider these suggestions as a minimum list of supplies. Even if you're not a mechanic and have no idea what you're doing with repairs or maintenance, having the tools listed may give someone else what they need to help you.

1. Emergency Kit
   a. Fire Extinguisher
   b. Car Escape Tool
   c. Trauma/First Aid Kit
2. Tools
   a. Wrench Set (Standard and Metric)
   b. Pliers
   c. Screwdrivers (Flathead and Phillips)
   d. Hammer
   e. Wire Cutters
   f. Duct Tape
   g. Flashlight (With Extra Batteries)
   h. Jumper Cables
   i. Window Scraper

j.   Military Entrenching Tool / Camp Shovel
3.   Parts and Fluids
     a.   Hose Clamps
     b.   Belts
     c.   Hoses
     d.   Fuse Kit
     e.   Coolant
     f.   3 Quarts of Oil
4.   Tire
     a.   Spare Tire
     b.   Jack
     c.   Tire Iron with cheater bar
     d.   Fix-A-Flat
     e.   Tire Pressure Gauge
     f.   Tire Repair Kit
5.   Personal Protection
     a.   Gloves
     b.   Eye Protection
     c.   Blanket
6.   Signaling
     a.   Brightly colored bandana
     b.   Orange Reflective Vest
     c.   Road Flares or Emergency Triangles
7.   Charger for cell phone 2 spare charging cables for your phone and 1 extra charging cable for another brand (Android to Apple or Apple to Android)
8.   Food
     a.   2 Gallons of Water
     b.   Granola Bars
9.   Roadside Assistance Card

Blackout kit

A power outage is most likely the event many of us will face the most frequently, yet most people do not have anything other than a couple of flashlights that we may or may not be able to find put away. Honestly, by assembling a simple blackout kit, you can turn an annoyance into something that you can get through with little difficulty and possibly even enjoy it.

Your blackout kit should contain all the things that'll get you through a power outage at home safely. Though a blackout kit should be personalized to the needs of the specific person, there are essential items that everyone should have on hand, beginning with your flashlights, batteries, and first aid kits.

Container: Every kit needs to begin with what you are going to use to store it in. You need to keep your items in one centralized location so you can find everything you need in the event of an emergency. This container may be a duffle bag, storage bin, or anything in between.

Batteries: You will have numerous items in your kit that take batteries, and while it is not wise to store those items with the batteries in them as this will lead to corrosion, you should have a few sets of batteries for each and every item in your case. I also keep a couple spare external cell phone batteries in my kit.

Emergency Radio: You will need to know what is going on, and anything that is being said about the incident. It is crucial to have an emergency radio to listen to these alerts. You can also use this to pass the time by listening to music.

Emergency tool: You may have to turn off the utilities, and for that reason, it is crucial to keep an emergency tool in your kit, so it is easy to get to.

Headlamp: A headlamp will give you a hand free option allowing you to work with both hands while having light available. A good headlamp should be your first choice as a light source.

Flashlight: Everyone knows the importance of a good flashlight. This should be more powerful than your headlamp.

Chem Lights: These can be very useful in lighting an area and can be fun for the kids to. You can change the mood of the situation by giving a couple of chem-lights to your kids.

Camp lantern: This is an excellent option for families. This will allow you to be in a lighted space without having to have all the flashlights on facing each other.

Portable Fan: While the above will give you lighting, a portable fan will keep you cool. During the summer heat, having battery-powered fans on hand can make a big difference.

Comfort Items: There are a few items that, while not life-sustaining, are still crucial for the wellbeing of yourself and your group. These include things to keep your family entertained, such as:

1. Puzzles and games
2. Deck of cards
3. Books
4. Video games
5. Audiobooks
6. Additional external batteries for cell phones
7. Power strip and extension cords
8. Candies and snacks

Class 4 (Construction materials)

When planning for an emergency, whether you plan on leaving or staying, you will want to do the work necessary to get your home ready for the crisis. This will protect you if you plan on remaining or help ensure you do everything required to protect your property so it can be returned to.

You will want to have materials before any run on stores that may take place to obtain those supplies. Depending on what your most significant threats will be, decide what building materials you should purchase. Construction Materials will include plywood sandbags or equivalents items.

Not only should you ensure that materials such as plywood and sandbags are on hand to help you protect your home during the event, but there are also steps you should take long before any of these events take place.

Stock up on plywood and sandbags

You will want plenty of plywood, sandbags, fasteners, and any other construction materials you know you use during the storm season as an affordable solution to protect windows and glass doors without shutters from projectiles. Stock up on plywood before the storm season begins to avoid that last-minute rush to the hardware store. You should store the plywood in a location where it is protected from the elements when not being used. A shed or garage works great.

Class 8 (Medical equipment)

Medical Kit or First Aid Kit

Call it a Medical Kit or First Aid Kit; it doesn't matter what you call it. It should have the supplies that you need when you need them. For this section, I will be using the term Medical Kit and breaking it down into a trauma, minor injury, medication, and support/comfort item section.

You will want to divide your kit into these categories to ensure you have your items when you need them, and they are easy to get to. Trauma supplies are typically required in more urgent scenarios than minor injury and comfort items.

So, make sure to keep these items stored in an easily accessible part of your medical kit.

Separating the compartments may be as easy as using the existing compartments of your bag. Or you may need to do a little more work. In that case, I recommend using stuff sacks and zip lock bags to keep your bag organized.

Trauma Kit

Trauma kits are meant to deal with significant injuries keeping your patient alive until a higher level of medical care can be reached. Hopefully, you never need one, but it's better to have and not need it than to need it but not have it. In building this kit, you will want to start with a bag. Then fill it with the medical gear you need to patch a severe injury. Trauma is one of those areas where your knowledge will be more important than what you have in your bag. That is why I recommend everyone take classes and become an EMT.

In general, the medical equipment that makes up the trauma kits can be broken down into the following areas:

Personal protective equipment (PPE): This should include gloves, masks, and eye protection. I would also recommend having shoe coverings as a just in case item. You will want to protect your footwear from body fluids that could soak through.

Patient assessment tools: The tools used to assess the patient's vital signs, including a stethoscope, blood pressure cuff, micropulse oximeter, thermometer, and CO_2 monitor.

Stop the Bleed supplies: These are tools designed to stop bleeding or seal off penetrating trauma. These items should include:
Hemostatic dressings of various sizes (Quik Clot, Celox)
An assortment of dressings ranging from 4x4s and 5x9s to ABD
Bandage wraps (4" and 6") Kling Roll gauze, Ace wraps, etc.
Israeli Bandages
Heavy-duty medical tape 1" and 2 "
Chest seals

Tourniquets

Airway/breathing management: Based on your training, these can range from a simple nasopharyngeal or oropharyngeal airway to potentially a full airway management pack. Equipment may include the following:
Basic airway stabilization. This may consist of oral and nasal airways, a pocket mask, and a manual suction device such as V-Vac
Collapsible bag valve mask (Cyclone Pocket)
Chest decompression supplies
More invasive airway control, such as endotracheal intubation or supraglottic airways

Patient transport system: In most cases, you will wait for an ambulance to arrive, but in some cases, such as being out in the woods or during a large-scale disaster, this might not be realistic or quick. For these incidents, you may need to self-transport or move to a location where the ambulance can reach you. A soft "roll-up" stretcher in your pack may be ideal for these situations.

INDIVIDUAL FIRST-AID KITS (IFAK)

In addition to what is in your trauma kit, each member of your group should carry and trained in the use of an Individual First Aid Kit (IFAK). This kit should be easily accessible at all times.

Equipment might include:

PPE (gloves, mask, eye protection)

A small pocket mask, NPA, OPA

Trauma scissors

1 or 2 tourniquets (SWAT-T, CAT)

Chest decompression kit

2-3 trauma dressings (Israeli type)

4-6 hemostatic dressings

2-3 open chest seal (Bolin, Hyfin, Asherman)

4 roller gauze, compression bandages

1 heavy-duty 2" tape (e.g., NARP Gecko tape)

1 personal care kit (PCK) that includes
medications, sunscreen, insect repellant, and/or
contact lens supplies

Minor Injury Kit

Materials for minor injuries, blisters, and
skincare will be your most commonly requested
item, with the most frequent of these being a
Band-Aid. Having a readily available supply of
assorted bandages is a must. Also, maintain
minor wound cleaning tools and topical antibiotic
ointment. Have a good assortment of 1" and 2"
breathable and non-breathable tape. Tools
such as tweezers, small scissors, and
wound/eye irrigation supplies should have a
place in the kit. Your kit should include:

2 absorbent compress dressings (5 x 9 inches)
adhesive bandages (assorted sizes)

1 adhesive cloth tape (10 yards x 1 inch)

5 antibiotic ointment

1 emergency blanket

1 instant cold compress

2 pair of nonlatex gloves (size: large)

2 hydrocortisone ointment packets (approximately 1 gram each)

1 3 in. gauze roll (roller) bandage

1 roller bandage (4 inches wide)

5 3 in. X 3 in. sterile gauze pads

5 gauze pads (4 x 4 inches)

Oral thermometer (non-mercury/non-glass)

2 triangular bandages

Tweezers

Ortho/sports equipment: Orthopedic injuries are common in training, and they happen on occasion during sports activities that your family may take part in. Skills such as taping, bracing, and in-field stabilization of orthopedic injuries should be a concentration for anyone who is going to be medically responsible for a group. SAM splints work well for most splinting needs.

Other items you may need might include cold packs and compression wraps.

Blister Kit: Blisters are a fact of life for a lot of people when hiking or running to prepare for these incidents you should keep a blister kit that includes; Molefoam, Moleskin, 2nd skin, and Medical tape.

Medication

Having an assortment of commonly used over the counter medications will keep minor ailments from progressing and prevent an onset of problems such as allergies. The over the counter medications I carry include:

Ibuprofen (Advil)

Acetaminophen (Tylenol)

Aspirin

Antihistamine

Imodium/Loperamide

Sudafed (*or equivalent*)

Throat lozenges

Bismuth tabs

Oral rehydration

Dramamine

Stool softener and/or Laxative

Antibiotic ointment

Hydrocortisone

Miconazole/Anti-fungal

Anti-Bacterial Bar Soap

You should also maintain a 90-day supply of any Prescription Medications that you have

Support/Comfort items

Small toy or puzzle: Keeping a toy or puzzle to win the attention of and comfort a child can be better than any medication.

Hand Sanitizer

Sunblock

Bug repellent

Vitamins

Keeping Your Kit Updated

So, the contents of your kit have been acquired and
organized, you have taken classes, and you are
ready to the best of your ability. But the work
doesn't stop there. Be sure to systematically check
your kit and replace items as needed. Remember
to look for expired medicine, container seal failures,
and leakage amongst your supplies. It helps
to unpack and repack your kit quarterly to take
stock and replace whatever needs replacing.

Conclusion

This might seem like a lot, and after reading this, I'm sure you are asking where to start and how are you ever going to get all this done. Just like anything else, this is accomplished by taking it one step at a time and knocking out one thing after another.

Now that you have read this, your next step should be to take a full inventory of your current supplies and capabilities. Most of us have more gear, equipment, and skills than we realize. Knowing where you sit, by having a good inventory of what you currently have, will prevent you from buying something you don't need. It also helps you sort through the junk you don't need, allowing you to sell it and use that money to buy what you do need.

Next, establish a realistic prepping budget based on how much you can safely spend on prepping.

Build your supplies when you can, may mean buying one extra can or box of food when you go to the grocery store, then start with one can. Even buying that one additional box of food regularly will add up quickly.

If you're short on funds, compensate by building your knowledge. Those who gain experience will be far better off than those who rely solely on gear they bought. There are advantages to being able to stockpile food, water, and some necessary survival supplies, but these supplies will only be increased with knowledge on how to use them to their best.

To be able to count on your knowledge, you need to run through your techniques in several scenarios and environments. The more you train in real-world situations, the more likely you will be able to perform your skills when it really matters.